Monument to Departed Worth

ENGLISH BIOGRAPHY
IN THE EARLY
NINETEENTH CENTURY

1801–1838

JOSEPH W. REED, JR.

NEW HAVEN AND LONDON   YALE UNIVERSITY PRESS   1966

Frontispiece from: THE LIFE OF ADMIRAL LORD NELSON,
Birmingham, Thomas Martin, 1805.

TO KIT

PREFACE

The early nineteenth century was not (as it was for autobiography) a golden age for biography. It is more notable for quantity of production than quality of workmanship, more significant for suppression than revelation, more noted for rules and checks on development than for biographical innovation. Because of the nature of the period a study of the biographies of 1801–38 necessarily tends more to evaluation than to appreciation.

A study of the trends and production of any genre in the infancy of the machine press would be justified for its relevance to social history alone, but this is also the period which produced two powerful biographies (Southey's *Nelson* and Lockhart's *Scott*) and one glorious failure (Moore's *Byron*) that merit both attention in their own right and investigation of their background in lesser biographies. In addition, two significant biographical theorists (James Field Stanfield and Thomas Carlyle) inform this background with some surprisingly sound artistic ideals.

Donald A. Stauffer's exhaustive studies of English biography[1]

1. *English Biography to 1700* (Cambridge, Mass., 1930) and *The Art of Biography in Eighteenth Century England* (2 vols. Princeton, 1941). In further references to the eighteenth-century title, Stauffer is used as cue title. Place of publication is London throughout unless otherwise noted.

vii

were carried to 1800. The century which follows has to be judged through portions of survey histories of biography.[2] There are important questions posed and left unanswered by these surveys, and I attempt to deal with some of these. I set out to continue Stauffer's work up to the accession of Victoria but continued through the end of 1838 in order to include Lockhart's *Scott*. This study takes a split view: treatment of some contemporary issues, some contemporary theory, and critiques of the three most significant biographies—Southey's *Nelson*, Moore's *Byron*, and Lockhart's *Scott*. The study ends with some rudimentary principles for the criticism of the art of biography —my conclusions on the problems of dealing with the aesthetics of an imperfect art. The principles are, of course, deeply rooted in the three individual critiques which precede them, but they are offered in an attempt to outline the problems of biographical criticism in general.

The approach is to biography as a phenomenon of its times, and the result perhaps tends to illustrate how inadequately literary history explains the phenomenal appearance of masterpieces. Literary history sets up rules and makes final observations; the best biographies deny both.

My first debt is to Frederick W. Hilles, under whose direction this study was begun as a Yale dissertation. He read the manuscript at every point in its progress, made available his personal library, argued, criticized, encouraged, and prodded me for several years. Donald A. Gallup advised me in the preparation of the check-list of biographies published, a first step in the

2. Waldo H. Dunn, *English Biography* (1916); William R. Thayer, *The Art of Biography* (New York, 1920); Harold Nicolson, *The Development of English Biography* (New York, 1928); John A. Garraty, *The Nature of Biography* (New York, 1957). Other critical studies utilizing the historical background but containing no chronological survey are James C. Johnston's *Biography: The Literature of Personality* (New York, 1927) and Dwight Durling and William Watt, *Biography: Varieties and Parallels* (New York, 1941). Edgar Johnson's *One Mighty Torrent* (New York, 1937) has a chronological organization, but considers the letters of the Romantic poets to be the most representative "biography" of the early nineteenth century.

dissertation that made the critical sections possible. James L. Clifford, Alexander Cowie, E. Talbot Donaldson, Richard L. Greene, Benjamin C. Nangle, and Frederick A. Pottle have read the manuscript and offered detailed and valued suggestions. Harriet Chidester, Rosalie Colie, George R. Creeger, Charles Feidelson, Benjamin F. Huston, Alvin B. Kernan, Richard M. Ohmann, Robert A. Smith, and Warren H. Smith have made suggestions and answered specific questions. The Yale Edition of the Private Papers of James Boswell has permitted the use of several manuscripts and the quotation of one passage from Boswell's journal. The Yale University Library has permitted the publication of passages from the unpublished Cadell correspondence; its splendid biographical collection and its periodical collection, together with that of the Olin Memorial Library at Wesleyan, made this study possible. I have also been assisted by Wesleyan's faculty research grants.

To all these and to all who typed and proofread (especially Mrs. Elizabeth German and Mrs. David B. Colby) my thanks. My wife criticized, listened, encouraged, and devised a system of proofreading which has yet to be properly recognized elsewhere. All mistakes and oversights are, of course, my own.

J. W. R., Jr.

Middletown, Connecticut
January 1964

CONTENTS

Preface   vii

1 Boswell and After   3

2 Biography as Example   27

3 Dignity and Suppression   38

4 Higher Criticism: Stanfield and Carlyle   66

5 Southey's *Nelson*   83

6 Moore's *Byron:* Myth in a Mold   102

7 Lockhart's *Scott*   127

8 Some Principles   154

   Bibliography   167

   Index   171

ENGLISH BIOGRAPHY
IN THE EARLY
NINETEENTH CENTURY

*He first ascertains . . . the date and place of the proposed
individual's birth, his parentage, trade, appointments, and the
titles of his works (the date of his death you already know from
the newspapers): this serves as a foundation for the edifice.
He then goes through his writings, and all other writings where
he or his pursuits are treated of, and whenever he finds a passage
with his name in it, he cuts it out, . . . and the building now proceeds
apace. Stone is laid on the top of stone, just as it comes to hand;
a trowel or two of biographic mortar, if perfectly convenient,
being perhaps spread in here and there, by way of cement; and so
the strangest pile suddenly arises; amorphous, pointing every way
but to the zenith—here a block of granite, there a mass of pipe-
clay; till the whole finishes, when the materials are finished—
and you leave it standing to posterity, like some miniature
Stonehenge, a perfect architectural enigma.*
                —THOMAS CARLYLE, in *Edinburgh Review, 46,* 177–78.

CHAPTER ONE

BOSWELL AND AFTER

England expects every driveller to do his Memorabilia.

—JOHN GIBSON LOCKHART [1]

With the example of the masterpiece of biography immediately available to it in a number of editions, biography in the early nineteenth century moved instead in the direction of the jerry-built hodgepodge Carlyle describes. Were biographical failures of the period, as Waldo H. Dunn suggests, [2] failures to realize the potential of the "Boswell formula"? Had the secret to the formula been lost, or did biographers even strive to imitate the formula at all? Why did Lockhart decline to "Boswellize" Scott?

Masterpieces of biography seem to be more significantly atypical than typical of the period which produces them, and a coherent line of literary development can more frequently be traced through bad works than through good, but there were better reasons than these for the failure to follow Boswell's lead.

A concrete indicator of Boswell's reputation in the nineteenth century is readily available in the publication of John Wilson Croker's edition of the *Life of Johnson* in 1831. Croker was of such importance and aroused such strong feelings himself that

1. In review of a group of autobiographies, *Quarterly Review*, 35 (1827), 149; ascribed to Lockhart by Marion Lochhead, *John Gibson Lockhart* (1954), p. 190.
2. *English Biography* (1916), pp. 157–80.

3

the edition was widely reviewed, perhaps more extensively (certainly more prejudicially) than Boswell's original had been.[3]

Croker himself, although his respect for Boswell as a recorder and patient chronicler knows no bounds, is more reserved in estimating his art. He finds Boswell's narratives "written with good sense, in an easy and perspicuous style, and without (which seems odd enough) any palpable imitation of Johnson."[4] But he seems determined to withhold judgment on the strictly artistic merit of the *Life*. He opens his preface with a mild disclaimer: "It were superfluous to expatiate on the merits, at least as a source of amusement, of Boswell's LIFE. . . . Whatever doubts may have existed as to the prudence or the propriety of the *original* publication—however naturally private confidence was alarmed, or individual vanity offended, the voices of criticism and complaint were soon drowned in the general applause. And no wonder—the work combines within itself the four most entertaining classes of writing—biography, memoirs, familiar letters, and that assemblage of literary anecdotes which the French have taught us to distinguish by the termination *Ana*."[5] The statement contains an implicit condescension toward the genre that is unfortunately typical of the early nineteenth century: Croker's temperate reservation ("at least as a source of amusement") is almost high praise. The critics of the period in general refused to acknowledge the art of the biographer; if there was an art to biography at all, it was the subject's art in designing his life. The second sentence sums up a reaction against eighteenth-century minutiae which manifested itself as the "doctrine of dignity."[6] The third completes the evasion of aesthetic judgment, fragmenting Boswell's *Life* into four genres, thus neatly avoiding the question of unity, which

---

3. For another view of Boswell's relationship to nineteenth-century biography, see Francis R. Hart, "Boswell and the Romantic Biographers," in *ELH*, 27 (1960), 44. Hart uses much of the same material covered in this chapter but arrives at different conclusions.

4. Croker's edition (1831), *1*, xiii.

5. Ibid., *1* [iii].

6. See below, Chapter 3.

is a first step in the recognition of art. Taken as a whole, the statement is representative of the nineteenth-century attitude toward Boswell's work; that it was regrettable to pry so, and to publish the results of such pryings; that once published it might be amusing, but never art.

The reviewers echoed the editor's reservations (with varying opinions about the usefulness of editing Boswell at all). At their best, they indicated Boswell's capacity to "delight" and his "readable" qualities. At their worst, they admired the reflection of Johnson in the mirror and ignored, vilified, or denigrated the mirror itself. The worst was, of course, Thomas Babington Macaulay's review in the *Edinburgh*.[7] His animadversions are too well known to be repeated here. The persistent misconception he so powerfully fostered (some of its effect is with us still) is perhaps the most damaging misconception of biography: that the subject of the biography is the artist; the biographer but sets down what he sees in the most direct manner possible. If the glass of the biographer is clear, then the biography will succeed. Macaulay (and many of his critical colleagues) considers only the biographer's labors: the collection, annotation, and transcription—never the creation: planning, organization, selection, or design. That Macaulay admired Boswell's work is clear, but it was an admiration which could scarcely inspire imitation of Boswell or repetition of his formula for success. According to Macaulay, his imitator would have to become "servile and impertinent,—shallow and pedantic,—a bigot and a sot,—bloated with family pride,"[8] and have snagged, to boot, the literary arbiter of an age as a subject.

The *Monthly* reviewer (as usual) was more pedestrian. He had a sounder view of biography, but perhaps as low an opinion of its art.

It is not to be denied, that even to the generations now arrived at maturity, that production, however delightful in itself, as the record of Johnson's style of conversation, and of the turn

7. *Edinburgh Review, 54* (1831), 1 ff.
8. Ibid., pp. 16–17.

of his thoughts, had already lost a very considerable portion of its interest, in consequence of our ignorance of the characters of many persons therein mentioned, of our inability to fill up the blanks which Boswell intentionally introduced, and to understand many of the allusions which he left unexplained. These characters . . . Mr. Croker has supplied; these blanks he has very frequently filled up; and these allusions he has for the most part rendered intelligible. . . . He has succeeded . . . in arresting the progress which one of the most entertaining memoirs in our language, was making toward the regions, not indeed of oblivion, but of obscurity. . . . In its present shape, Boswell's Life may be considered as one of the most complete and interesting publications in our language.[9]

Lockhart in the *Quarterly* echoed Macaulay's paradox, but only commented on Boswell as a puzzling enigma instead of making him the occasion of a literary law: "Never did any man tell a story with such liveliness and fidelity, and yet contrive to leave so strong an impression that he did not himself understand it . . . unconscious, all the while, of the real gist and bearing of the facts he is narrating."[1] That which remains a mystery can hardly be imitated.

All of which may lead to the false assumption that everyone was as puzzled by Boswell's work as the critics were, or that biographers waited patiently for the critics to evolve the pattern so that they might then imitate it. These statements do, however, represent an attitude toward a specifically literary reputation in the period, and the fact remains that there was no large-scale attempt to imitate the whole "Boswell formula" in the early part of the century. Imitation would doubtless have been more likely had Boswell been universally praised as an artist of biography, or had it been widely held that biography was an art at all.

That portion of the "formula" distinctly original with

9. *Monthly Review*, IV, 2 (1831), 453–54, 464.
1. *Quarterly Review*, 46 (1831), 8.

Boswell—the fully recorded conversation (or the dramatically rendered conversational scene)—was copied. Perhaps the systematic recording of conversation may be considered a logical extension of the organized anecdote or of -*ana,* but it is clear that Boswell made an art of what was not much more than an accidental practice when he found it. Even though imitation of this much of the "formula" is not sufficient evidence to demonstrate confidently a "school of Boswell," the imitations inform an assessment of Boswell's nineteenth-century reputation.

Of the conscious imitators, perhaps the most original, the truest to the form, and the most successful was Barry Edward O'Meara, an English doctor assigned to the personal service of Napoleon in his final exile on St. Helena. His book (*Napoleon in Exile; or, A Voice from St. Helena. The Opinions and Reflections of Napoleon on the Most Important Events of His Life and Government, in His Own Words,* 1822) attempts no more than it can accomplish, never pretends to a greater scope than O'Meara's acquaintance of a year justifies, but at some points approaches the achievement of clear and perfectly rendered presence. O'Meara is no Boswell. He does not have Boswell's faith in his Johnson (a faith certainly essential to the act of recording so much), and he never achieves the intimacy with the former emperor that would make his book a great moment in biography. He also lacks Boswell's sense of the importance of minor characters in conversational dramas, and is entirely too interested in *what* Napoleon is saying to be totally objective or totally dramatic.

The book does have moments, however, which show that Boswell's was not a lost art. Some of Napoleon's reminiscences have the power to re-create what Napoleon had been—notably his explanation of the Russian campaign (although its conclusion is perhaps more Werther than Bonaparte):

I myself remained in the Kremlin until surrounded with flames. The fire advanced, seized the Chinese and India warehouses, and several stores of oil and spirits, which burst forth in flames and overwhelmed every thing. I then retired

7

to a country house of the emperor Alexander's, distant about a league from Moscow, and you may figure to yourself the intensity of the fire, when I tell you, that you could scarcely bear your hands upon the walls or the windows on the side next to Moscow, in consequence of their heated state. It was the spectacle of a sea and billows of fire, a sky and clouds of flame; mountains of red rolling flames, like immense waves of the sea, alternately bursting forth and elevating themselves to skies of fire, and then sinking into the ocean of flame below. Oh, it was the most grand, the most sublime, and the most terrific sight the world ever beheld!! *Allons, Docteur.*[2]

The central conflict of the book, between Napoleon and the British governor, Sir Hudson Lowe, makes the closest approach to first-rate biography. Here again, O'Meara's carefully qualified and subdued hero-worship of the emperor and his corresponding hatred of Napoleon's British jailer keeps this from being as good as it might have been. Here and there Sir Hudson Lowe emerges as an opponent worthy of O'Meara's Napoleon, but too often he is only a caricature of frustrations, prejudices, and too blatantly rendered neurotic quirks. The second volume becomes preoccupied with Napoleon's physical symptoms, and the book trails off into another genre, that of the authentic deathbed account.

O'Meara's method was a variation upon Boswell's—not so thoroughly organized, but in a way made more self-conscious by O'Meara's precautions for the accuracy and the security of his transcript.

I spoke as little and listened as attentively as I could, seldom interposing, except for the purpose of leading to those facts on which I wished for information. To my memory, though naturally retentive, I did not entirely trust; immediately on retiring from Napoleon's presence, I hurried to my chamber and carefully committed to paper the topics of conversation, with, so far as I could, the exact words used. Where I had

2. O'Meara, *1*, 196. The last two words were Napoleon's dismissal of O'Meara for the evening.

the least doubt as to my accuracy, I marked it in my journal, and by a subsequent recurrence to the topic, when future opportunities offered, I satisfied myself; this, although I have avoided them as much as possible, may account for some occasional repetitions, but I have thought it better to appear sometimes tedious, than ever to run the risk of a mistatement.[3]

Since the whole project was frowned upon by the British government, O'Meara took elaborate precautions to get the copy out—perhaps the most zanily elaborate in the history of biography:

As nothing which could possibly occur at St. Helena would have surprised me, I determined to place its contents [the journal's] at least beyond the power of that spoliation which afterwards was perpetrated on some of my other property. Having purchased in the island, a machine for that purpose, I transmitted at intervals the portions copied to a friend on board one of his majesty's ships in the roads, who forwarded them as opportunities occurred, to Mr. Holmes of Lyon's Inn, Napoleon's respectable agent in London. The entire of this copy Mr. Holmes duly received some time previous to my return to England, as appears below by his own authentication, and part of the silver paper manuscript as he received it, I have deposited with my publisher for the satisfaction of the sceptical. Thus, for the authenticity of the following conversations the reader has the guarantees, first, of the undoubted opportunities afforded me, 2ndly, of their having been taken on the spot, 3rdly, of their having been transmitted at the moment, and 4thly, of the original document itself, authenticated by the person to whom it had been consigned and now submitted to general inspection.[4]

The whole book would have been more successful as biography had O'Meara been less attentive to authenticity. He failed through inclusiveness—where Boswell seemed to err, but where we know now selection and shaping were always at work.

3. O'Meara, *1*, xii.
4. Ibid., pp. xii–xiii.

O'Meara "thought that every fragment of such a mind should be preserved to history,"[5] a sentiment which clearly arrays him in the ranks of the indefatigable savers of scraps from the stream of time. As it is, it is still an interesting experiment in method with some brilliant passages, and the most successful Boswellian dramatization of this period.

Of the other ventures in this method, perhaps the less said the better. Thomas Medwin's *Journal of the Conversations of Lord Byron* . . . (1824) is certainly an attempt at Boswellization, but its similarity in method only demonstrates how important to Boswell's method was his absolute honesty and accuracy. Devotion to the truth was apparently not Medwin's strong point: his book inspired a series of corrections, notes, and defenses.[6] The conversations, as published, do have some of the zest and swiftness of Byron's letters, but the forming hand (in the good sense) is lacking. The conversations seldom come to life as Boswell's do. Medwin, like O'Meara, was much too interested in *what* Byron was saying to dramatize successfully the full force and the give-and-take of a lively conversation.

Had Macaulay's principle been true, H. N. Coleridge should have produced in Coleridge's *Table-Talk* (1835) a biography second only to Boswell's. Macaulay was wrong, and Coleridge constructs a collection of summaries with all the fascination of a two-volume table of contents. He disclaims kinship to Boswell early in the book.

A cursory inspection will show that these volumes lay no claim to be ranked with Boswell's in point of dramatic interest. Coleridge differed not more from Johnson in every characteristic of intellect, than in the habits and circumstances of his life, during the greatest part of the time in which I was intimately conversant with him. He was naturally very fond of society, and continued to be so to the last; but

5. Ibid., pp. xiv–xv.

6. *Exposure of the Mis-statements Contained in Captain Medwin's Pretended 'Conversations with Lord Byron'* (1824); John Murray's *Notes on Captain Medwin's Conversations of Lord Byron* (1824); and *Captain Medwin Vindicated from the Calumnies of the Reviewers* by Vindex [pseud.] (1825).

the almost unceasing ill health with which he was afflicted, after fifty, confined him for many months in every year to his own room, and, most commonly, to his bed. He was then rarely seen except by single visiters; and few of them would feel any disposition upon such occasions to interrupt him, whatever might have been the length or mood of his discourse. And indeed, although I have been present in mixed company, where Mr. Coleridge has been questioned and opposed, and the scene has been amusing for the moment— I own that it was always much more delightful to me to let the river wander at its own sweet will, unruffled by aught but a certain breeze of emotion which the stream itself produced.[7]

Coleridge at least understands Boswell and knows the difference between the book he is constructing and the *Life*. But underlying his final metaphor is more than a hint that he considered Boswell's treatment of Johnson an affront to the intellect of the great man—meddling, in other words, to which he refused to stoop.

All who attempt to imitate Boswell give a slight bow in his direction, but it is apparent that their inclination to follow him is not as strong as other aims. The imitation is only of a part of Boswell, never of the whole, and even the part seems to hold an allegiance to a principle which is something less than (and certainly different from) Boswell's ideal of complete dramatization of conversational scenes. In the imitation, *what* the subject said is more important than how he said it, or the conversation in which it was said—more important even than what it revealed of the man who said it. This is a survival of certain biographical trends of the eighteenth century before Boswell: the tendency to see biography as an ordering and filling-in of all available autobiographical documents; the great principle of preservation—saving every scrap in blind faith that any material is worth saving, all material equally valuable; and a

7. *Specimens of the Table-Talk of the Late Samuel Taylor Coleridge* (1835), *1*, xii–xiii.

developing interest in individual character and personality evidenced in historiography. Together these trends form a juncture between eighteenth- and nineteenth-century biography.

Donald A. Stauffer has traced the history and development of the biographical anecdote in the eighteenth century and has indicated the great popularity of anecdotes after 1750.[8] Certainly Boswell's method involved the integration of anecdote with his other materials, but the dominance of anecdote in the late eighteenth and early nineteenth centuries is surely more profitably regarded as a continuation of the general taste for a species of material than as imitation of Boswell. Stauffer feels that some of the reasons for the anecdote's growth in popularity may be seen in the eighteenth century's rising antiquarian interest. Collections of anything and everything—historical cabinets, reconstructive architecture and design, the great libraries—were all manifestations of the mood to value whatever could lead the thoughts into the past. Chatterton, Macpherson, and, more recently, William Henry Ireland had demonstrated the hypnotic effect which an artificially yellowed manuscript or an antiqued phrase could have upon the reading public. Letters, anecdotes, and bits of conversation possessed, in the hands of effective literary artists such as Horace Walpole, Boswell, or Selwyn, a potent power to illuminate the past which simple narration of events could not match.

The early nineteenth century, unfortunately, did not distinguish matter from manner. The publication of anecdote had moved so far in development, independent of the other genres it customarily supported, that it was on the verge of becoming a genre itself. Anecdotes could be living moments of the past: an attempt had to be made to salvage all such ephemeral moments, which disappeared so rapidly when the participants passed from the scene, and when living human memory failed. Anecdote-salvagers became like German literary historians, not so much interested in the worth of the material as they were in the hole into which the material might be stuffed, in the

8. Stauffer, *1*, 485–95.

continuing construction of the perfect monument of the past. A popular rhetorical image was the stream of human memory, from which the fragile refuse of the past had to be plucked before it was swept beneath the surface: "But the pen of biography, independent of the impulse of general curiosity which calls it instantly into exercise, must seek and arrange its materials upon the spur of the moment, whilst minor and more minute events are floating on the stream of living recollection, ere they pass into the ocean of forgetfulness."[9] William Bayle Bernard, assigned the task of editing his father's autobiography, twisted the figure. Publication was the stream; he resolved to cast upon it only the worthwhile portions of his father's narrative (that is, the anecdotes).[1] Minor writers, eager to do their part on behalf of total recall, reminisced and recollected over the newspapers and recollections of other writers, salvaging again ephemera which had been saved already. Memories and recollections were, after all, in the public domain. Contemporary critics were almost unanimously indignant at the flood of repetitive memoirs that resulted.[2] Charles Bucke, one of the

9. *George the Third, His Court, and Family* (1820), p. [v].

1. "At his death, the MS. fell into my hands, to be consigned either to the flames or the press. Convinced that it contained a great body of theatrical anecdotes, which had failed to float down the stream, I did not consider it my duty to oppose the Son to the Editor, and prevent their diffusion . . . among my own generation. I have accordingly subtracted the same, with no more personal detail than was absolutely necessary to their historical connection, and now present them." John Bernard, *Retrospections*, edited by W. B. Bernard (1830), "The editor's advertisement," pp. iv–v.

2. "This is one of those gossiping, garrulous, trifling, chit-chat memoirs, which have abounded in our literary market of late years. An elderly gentleman recollects a few anecdotes of eminent persons, which he happens to repeat in the presence of some one who tells him that they are really worth preserving, and that he might moreover get a very good price for them, if he could spin them out into a volume or two. The bargain is made. Straight he goes to work in turning over his long forgotten, dusty papers. These renew the memory of other incidents: some more he collects from his friends and from the magazines and newspapers of bye-gone days, and so he makes up the requisite number of pages, and calls them his Memoirs." Review of the *Memoirs of Sir James Campbell* . . . (1832) in *Monthly Review*, IV, 5, 148.

more indefatigable salvagers of the national memory,[3] admits candidly in a preface that he applied a variation of this method to the composition of his life of Akenside: "Having formerly known two gentlemen, who had been intimately acquainted with him, I combined what I had heard them say of him with what was already known; and taking his works for a general guide . . . I have, I hope, been enabled to give a correct and, perhaps, not altogether an uninteresting outline of a virtuous and high-minded man."[4] A glance at a few of these volumes will convince the most skeptical reader that anecdotes on the loose, not organized within the design of biography or history, are about as attractive as multivolume sets of sermons. Conviction of the importance of such "scraps and pieces" to the body of the world's learning is but part of the great faith in the exhaustive compendium of all information—a faith which led ultimately to Lytton Strachey's blast at "those fat volumes."

Surviving from the eighteenth century, but coming into full force only in the nineteenth, was a historical formulation which emphasized the importance and power of the individual. J. B. Black, a twentieth-century historiographer, attributes a major turning-point to Voltaire. In *Essai sur les moeurs et l'esprit des nations,* Black sees an expression of Voltaire's opposition "to any mechanical interpretation of history that conflicted with the freedom of man to determine his own destiny."[5] Personality and character assert themselves over the illogical, nonhuman agents of causation.

> From time to time there arise great men, who gather up and incarnate in themselves the spirit of epochs. . . . They are the *demiurges de l'humanité,* the true heroes of the race. . . . Thus history is to be viewed as a struggle of rival and opposing forces . . . lit up and traversed periodically by human genius. In other words, there is intelligence presiding over

3. He compiled a number of compendia of anecdotes.
4. *On the Life, Writings, and Genius of Akenside* (1832), p. [v].
5. *The Art of History* (1926), p. 46.

the movements of society; but it is not the intelligence of Bossuet's supernatural Being: it is a plural intelligence with its seat on the earth. To the old historical monotheism has succeeded a historical polytheism.[6]

By the late eighteenth century, history was more than geographic and economic causation or the blind progress of cyclic events. Personality was recognized as the force with which man attempted to condition his circumstances. There was more attention given to individual leaders, in a growing belief that the human mind and the character, will, and personality that shaped and directed it had the power to affect the course of history.

Carlyle's histories and biographies realized the logical extension of historical polytheism later in the century, but for the readers of the early nineteenth century there were compelling illustrations of the force of character and the power of personality moving among them, and moving nations with them. Napoleon, Nelson, and Wellington were persuasive examples, the French Revolution an overwhelming demonstration of the theory.

Reorientation of the historian's view forced upon biography an important historical function already recognized in the eighteenth century. Stauffer, in his discussion of antiquarian lives,[7] cites Matthew Maty's statement in the *Memoirs of His Life* (1777) as representative of the eighteenth-century estimate of the historical value of memoirs:

It is from the number and variety of private memoirs and the collision of opposite testimonies, that the judicious reader is enabled to strike out light, and find his way through that darkness and confusion. . . . The characteristics of any country or age must be deduced from the separate characters of persons. . . . From the life of almost any one individual, but chiefly from the lives of such eminent men as seemed destined

6. Ibid., p. 44.
7. Stauffer, *1*, 231–54.

to enlighten or to adorn society, instructions may be drawn, suitable to every capacity, rank, age, or station.[8]

From this rather vague sense that personal memoirs contributed to, or were a source for, general history developed the nineteenth-century conviction that such memoirs or lives constituted an independent form of history, by and in themselves.

The treatment of biography as a branch of history had several attractions. Lives took on the added luster of educational literature when so dignified by association. Biographies, especially those of men in public life and of military figures, deserved more serious consideration when regarded as history: they took on "utility."[9] Idle curiosity about the details of private life (the nineteenth-century critic often attributed this motive to readers of biographies of which he did not approve) was not proper incentive for the reader, but, when shown to be history, biography was worthy of the attention of any serious reader eager for improvement: "It is sometimes started as a question, whether history or biography be the more improving study . . . but . . . biography, as it is the most interesting form of detached history, will often prove the most instructive and eligible mode as it regards political history; and with respect to illustrious individuals in private life, little needs be said to point out the usefulness of the candid and impartial biographer. It is in instances of this nature . . . that history becomes in a peculiar manner 'philosophy teaching by example.' "[1] This passage im-

8. *Memoirs of His Life, Tending to Illustrate the Civil, Literary, and Political History of His Time,* an essay prefaced to the *Works* of Lord Chesterfield (1777), pp. 2–3; quoted by Stauffer, *1,* 238–39.

9. The concept of "utility" was consistently applied to works which showed a way, set forth an example, or added to the published store of factual knowledge. There was no implication here, I believe, of the greatest good for the greatest number, but there was an implication that literature of all kinds had an obligation to contribute to the public education, the moral strength, and the aggregate learning of the nation. Works lacking this "utility" could be called "trash": they accomplished no worthwhile purpose.

1. Review of Mary Hays' *Female Biography* . . . (1802), *Monthly Review,* II, *43,* 92. The author is identified by Benjamin C. Nangle (*The Monthly*

plies a critical principle: biography is both attractive and valuable as a history of the times in miniature. A life is a microcosm of the great events of a period, reflected in the human (and hence more readily understandable) events, problems, and decisions of its subject. The biography of a public figure was even more attractive and valuable: "the record of the actions of an individual, indeed, but of an individual who was occupied with the destiny of nations; and while in some parts it attracts and amuses by the familiar incidents of private life, it aspires in others to the dignity of history."[2]

Biography at the same time retained its indirect historical function: lives were the mortar for the construction of general history, cementing great events with simpler, and more coherent actions: "It is to Biography that History owes those accessories which not only unite, but often illustrate, the greater events which she finds, though accurately recorded, yet imperfectly connected with the individuals who have been the most powerful, though not apparently the most active agents in their developement."[3] In the assertion of biography's historical function, as microcosm and as mortar, is implied a relationship of biography to history similar to that of anecdote to biography: individual character and action (biography) were to history what anecdotal vignettes were to the depiction of character in biography. The smaller elements represented the larger in microcosm; each illumined the other in a way that a simple narrative of events could not.

Nevertheless, with all the improvement and solid advance-

Review, 1790–1815, 1955, p. 257) as ?Man--g. The quotation at the end of the review, perhaps the most popular single quotation with reviewers of biography and writers of biographical prefaces ("History is philosophy teaching by examples") is from Bolingbroke's On the Study of History, letter 2. He identified the ultimate source as Dionysius of Halicarnassus.

2. Review of Macdiarmid's Lives of British Statesmen (1807), Monthly Review, II, 57 (1808), 1, written by Joseph Lowe and George Edward Griffiths (Nangle, pp. 26, 38–39, 159).

3. George the Third, His Court, and Family (1820), p. vi.

ment of learning which this view of biography offered, all three trends inherited from the eighteenth century moved biography farther and farther from art. The emphasis on autobiographical materials enforced the contention that a biographer could never know or render his subject as well as that subject could know and render himself. The faith in massive accumulation of anecdote as an independent genre reduced the incisive or significant anecdotal insight to the level of all anecdotes: substance was more important than treatment.

The acceptance of biography as a most "useful" branch of history submitted a genre that had evolved from belles lettres to a set of criteria and requirements which were not primarily aesthetic. All three trends emphasized the external functions of biography at the expense of the central core of biographical art: the image of one man as seen by another man, with a coherent design, organization, and unified effect of its own. Documents, compendia of anecdotes, and chronology (or, worse, the transformation of biography into a history of the times) were all enemies to selection, arrangement, and image. To paraphrase Geoffrey Scott, even as Boswell had no fear that other biographers might anticipate him, he need have had no fear of successful imitation. His successors were less than anyone aware that good biography was impossible.

Biography of the nineteenth century had troubles enough of its own, however, so that the burden of its failure could not be laid to distractions inherited from the eighteenth century. The most important, for it modified all other literary, intellectual, and social forces at work on biography, was the expansion of publishing that resulted from the first real improvement in the speed and facility of printing since Caxton: the Stanhope press and improvements upon it.[4] The advent of machine-made

4. The Stanhope press (circa 1800), the Koenig steam press (which began printing in England in 1811–12) and Cowper's (1818) and Applegarth's (1827) refinements of the Koenig press revolutionized printing (Henry R. Plomer, *A Short History of English Printing, 1476–1898*, 1900, pp. 282–85).

paper[5] completed a revolution which opened to publishers new possibilities of economy and consequent mass distribution. At the same time the Sunday School movement and a general extension of literacy in the middle and lower classes were producing thousands of new readers.[6] The Bible would not satisfy them for long.

Publishers were in an enviable position. Technological advances assured that supply could meet demand, and, at the same time, demand was expanding to meet supply's full potential. They rushed to realize the opportunities of this dream market. Economy of production not only permitted larger editions, but demanded more titles; expansion of publishing produced a corresponding expansion in writing. Publishers sought manuscripts from unknown writers, and writers searched the past and present for new subjects. Biography was inviting because it was deceptively easy to write. Once in possession of the materials, a writer could turn out a contemporary biography with less creative effort than was required for a bad novel. It was equally inviting to write the lives of men long dead; if they had already been treated in lives by their contemporaries, the old facts had only to be recast in the modern mold.

Consequently, by the beginning of the nineteenth century, life-writing had become a business. Lives were promised before the deathbed was cold, and the enterprising prospective biographer had to follow heavy on the wheels of the hearse if he expected to nab his subject. An aura of necrophilia always hangs about the edges of the genre. But as the popularity of biography increased, and publishing expanded so violently, immediate

5. The paper-making machines of Nicolas-Louis Robert (operative in England circa 1804) and of John Dickinson (1809) made available almost unlimited supplies of cheap paper (Dard Hunter, *Papermaking: The History and Technique of an Ancient Craft*, 2d ed. 1947, pp. 345–51).

6. The most concrete explanation for the spread of reading among the lower classes is L. E. Elliott-Binns' suggestion that Sunday School instruction enabled many and encouraged many more to read the Bible, and that "those who were induced to study the Bible would not make it their sole means of mental sustenance" (*The Early Evangelicals*, 1953, pp. 396–97).

composition and quick publication became the rule—even more so than in the eighteenth century's gallows biographies and deathbed accounts. Stock-jobbing of lives was conventional practice for even the most respectable publishers, and the competition for the cooperation of the decedent's family and for private papers frequently became more heated than competition for his manuscripts when alive.

A rich case in point is the negotiation of Thomas Cadell for a Life of William Pitt the Younger.[7] In 1809 Cadell contracted with John Gifford and Henry Redhead Yorke for a life of William Pitt ("or some such Title") to be jointly composed and written, "to form four large octavo volumes" (it eventually made only three).[8] Six years later Cadell wrote to George Tomline for a second life, to be composed from Tomline's more extensive manuscript holdings.

> The ample materials possessed by your Lordship and Mr. Rose together with the stores of one or 2 other of Mr. Pitt's most distinguished friends, which, if necessary, would doubtless be freely open to your joint influence, for such a purpose, would constitute a noble and most appropriate monument . . . which cannot, for a moment be considered as anticipated by the very inadequate and imperfect work of Mr. Gifford—[9] I am fully sensible that any thing which I could urge, in a merely commercial point of view, would not have the smallest influence with either your Lordship or Mr. Rose; yet it may not be improper for me to state . . . that we should be most happy in using every exertion in our power, towards pro-

7. The correspondence is in the Yale University Library, and consists of a fragmentary archive of the publishing house.

8. Undated contract, in the Cadell correspondence. Payment was £300 on publication, £400 four months later, £200 for the second edition, and £100 for the third.

9. Yorke is not listed on the title page, and has not been traced as co-author anywhere save the contract. He was perhaps a professional writer, brought in to facilitate matters. In 1812 he revised Berkenhout's version of Campbell's *Lives of the Admirals.*

moting the objects and interests of so important a publication.[1]

When the contract in the same year went to John Murray, however, Cadell was less hesitant in revealing his "purely commercial point of view."

From the character for respectability which our House has hitherto maintained as publishers, and from the means it possesses of promoting the circulation of new works, fully as powerful as the one selected upon this occasion, I cannot but flatter myself that the sale of your Lordship's Work would, if it had been committed to my care, have been attended with at least an equal degree of success as it will experience in the hands of its present publisher.[2]

Such enthusiasm on the part of publishers, needless to say, did not assure the best biographical opportunity to the best writer, nor did it allow for much selection of suitable writer for subject. In another instance, Thomas Campbell's name was advanced by the publisher as prospective author of a life of Sir Thomas Lawrence, with full knowledge that he would not complete the work, but in the hope that his name would command the greatest communication of material and documents, and perhaps scare away "the minor vagrants of the forest."[3]

One can almost overlook the quality of the mass of biographical production when contemplating its scope and facility. There was no dearth of great deaths: if it followed (as Macaulay implied) that the greater subject produced the greater biography, then this age might have seen glorious biography such as the literature had never known. Pitt and Fox, George III and George IV, Coleridge, Shelley, and Keats—the old order passed on, and a good percentage of the shortlived new order, too.

The major heroes of the age were, if anything, overtreated: 23 lives of Lord Nelson; 25 of Bonaparte (whose fascination for

1. Cadell to George Tomline, afterwards Pretyman, 2 Oct. 1815, copy in the Cadell correspondence, Yale.
2. Cadell to Tomline, 17 Feb. 1821.
3. See below, Chapter Three, p. 48 n.

English biographers was very much in evidence long before his death in 1821); and 30 biographical titles concerning Lord Byron. Luminaries of the century just past were not neglected: Burke, Goldsmith, and Garrick; Voltaire, Locke, and Hume; Wesley, Pitt the Elder, and Frederick the Great. Neither did the eager life-merchants neglect the lesser lights: Cowper, Akenside, and Hannah More; Kean, Kemble, and Mrs. Siddons; Heber, Watts, and Paley.

Biographical treatment was extended back toward (and perhaps beyond) the dawn of history: Cromwell, Shakespeare, Erasmus, Henry V, Charlemagne, Belisarius, St. Paul, Rachel, and Moses. The biographical method was even mistakenly applied to animals, and the battle against cruelty to brute creatures was waged by means of "biographies," "memoirs," and "anecdotes" of horses and donkeys, dogs and monkeys.[4]

4. Twenty-three titles containing anecdotes, memoirs, adventures, or biographies of sundry animals turn up in this period. Since they concern subhuman subjects, they do not really have a place in this study, but because they are somewhat more important than the bad jokes that they appear to be at first glance, I am loath to pass over them without comment. They fall into three groups: serious amateur studies of natural history (e.g. William Bingley's *Animal Biography; or, Anecdotes of the Lives, Manners, and Economy, of the Animal Creation, Arranged according to the System of Linnaeus*, 3 vols. 1803); anticruelty tracts (e.g. Capt. Thomas Brown's *Biographical Sketches and Authentic Anecdotes of Dogs, Exhibiting Instances of Their Instinct . . . with . . . a Copious Appendix on the . . . Treatment of Dogs*, Edinburgh, 570 pp., 1829); and juveniles, often not without overtones of the anticruelty tract (*Life and Death of a Monkey . . . A Tale for Young Persons*, 1814). There is one satire (Nathaniel Ogle's *Memoirs of Monkeys*, 152 pp., 1825), which substitutes beasts for types of men. There are also a few presumably authentic narratives of particular, individual pets (*The Life of Carlo, the Famous Dog of Drury-Lane Theatre. With His Portrait*, 1804), and, of course, a number of fanciful appreciations of nature (Mary Belson Elliott's *Rambles of a Butterfly*, 177 pp., 1819). Some of these titles (e.g. Mrs. Mary Pilkington's *The Sorrows of Caesar, or Adventures of a Foundling Dog*, 1813) reflect the current taste for novels rather than the vogue for biography. In the main, however, the wording of the titles, even as the wording used in titles of harmonies of the Gospels (*Memoirs of the Life and Doctrine of Christ*, 3 vols. 1804) is an indication of the great popularity of biography, on which the publishers relied to help sell these books.

The most striking characteristic of the scope of the subject matter, however, was the wave of biographical works devoted to the notably obscure. The great leveling which in the eighteenth century brought the tribute of biography to the common man continued. The feeling grew that distinction was only relative, after all. Had not Dr. Johnson himself justified the right of the most obscure to biographical attention?

I have often thought that there has rarely passed a life of which a judicious and faithful narrative would not be useful. For, not only every man has, in the mighty mass of the world, great numbers in the same condition with himself, to whom his mistakes and miscarriages, escapes and expedients, would be of immediate and apparent use; but there is such an uniformity in the state of man, considered apart from adventitious and separable decorations and disguises, that there is scarce any possibility of good or ill, but is common to human kind.[5]

Taking the great Doctor at his word, peripatetic life-writers filled the record with biographies of shadowy semi-celebrities and the prides of obscure families: Mary Ann Moore, the fasting woman of Tutbury; James Wilson, the blind poet; Charles Eulenstein, celebrated performer upon the jew's-harp; Joanna Southcott, would-be mother to rabbits; Rattenbury the smuggler; peddlers, maniacs, and eccentrics. And most numerous, of course, the worthy curates and rectors, their pious and zealous wives, principal secretaries of missionary societies, the mothers of esteemed memory, and the clouds of witness rising from the untimely graves of the children of happy memory, and equally happy death.

At first glance, the publication record seems to indicate a curiously split view of the role and proper function of biography: attention seems divided between the great heroes (victims of biographical overexposure) and the most obscure common men (for whom, in many instances, a single biography apiece constitutes overexposure). To realize the breadth of the

5. *Rambler*, no. 60, *Works* (1787), 5, 382–83.

coverage of available subjects, however, one has only to search for significant contemporary figures who were completely over-looked. In the field of letters, Keats comes first to mind; then Jane Austen (but she was, after all, a woman); even William Blake, enjoying little contemporary reputation, was the subject of a brief memoir which turns up in the dedication of Benjamin Heath Malkin's biography of his son.[6]

The biographers are representative of nearly every level of station or talent. There are a few noble authors, many rather competent professional biographers, a larger number of book-sellers' hirelings and bona fide hacks, and an even larger number of rank amateurs, unwilling to commit to the flames so in-teresting a heap of family papers, or pressed into service by zealous family or parish commemorators. Yet this majority of adequate, and totally incompetent, writers is strengthened by a number of first-rate men of letters: Scott, Southey, Hazlitt, Godwin, and Carlyle all produced biographies; Dickens edited an autobiography; Byron, Macaulay, and even Wordsworth were on hand to criticize the work of others.

In addition, biographical masterpieces were revived: an im-proved text of Cavendish's *Wolsey* was brought out; Walton's *Lives* and Johnson's *Lives of the Poets* were republished; Croker edited Boswell. Compilers pored over old biographies to pro-duce new works, and extracted, reworked, expurgated, or con-densed them for inclusion in collections, dictionaries,[7] and historical studies. At worst, such antiquarian zeal produced William Godwin's *Life of Chaucer* (1803), justly denounced by Robert Southey in the *Annual;*[8] at best, it brought the begin-nings of modern scholarly documentation and responsible his-torical inquiry, as in William Roscoe's *Life and Pontificate of Leo the Tenth* (1805), recognized in its own time as remark-able, and not completely superseded in our own. All these

6. *A Father's Memoirs of His Child,* [Thomas Williams Malkin], (Long-mans, 1806). The account of Blake is on pp. xviii–xli.

7. Twenty biographical dictionaries (in addition to the large number of collections of lives) were produced in the period.

8. *Annual Review* for 1803, 2, 464.

efforts served to consolidate existing biographical information, while benefiting from the public's apparently insatiable appetite[9] for new lives, new facts, and new anecdotes.

In spite of the continuing trends, the opening of the nineteenth century marked a breaking point in the history of the art of biography. No longer was the central concern of biography the interior man or the genesis and progress of character and personality. There were still some books—like Murphy's *Garrick* and Roberts' *Hannah More* (of which the faults are perhaps more of the eighteenth than of the nineteenth century)—which showed a continuation of these concerns. If the eighteenth century was, as Stauffer contends, the Golden Age of Biography, then it is clear that for a number of reasons this age had ended. The externals of life-writing had become more important than internal order. There was too great a concern with collection and exhaustive compendia, too little with the biographer's prerogatives of selection, arrangement, and timing. Where artistry is not called for, it seldom appears on its own.

But it was not quite the Dark Ages of biography either. Much was done in the exhaustive publication of documents and correspondences without which the twentieth-century biographer would be lost. In the midst of all our caviling at the nineteenth

9. The appetite for biography apparently exceeded the general expansion in publication. A good gauge of quantitative popularity may be found in the subscription family libraries, which were begun in the early part of the century and had become by 1838 a major publishing enterprise. Of thirty-seven of these serial sets found in the *English Catalogue*, lists were analyzed for twelve: *The Christian's Family Library, Constable's Miscellany, Edinburgh Cabinet Library, Family Library, Lardner's Cabinet Cyclopaedia, Lardner's Cabinet Library, Sacred Classics, Murray's Home and Colonial Library, Select Christian Authors, Smith's Souvenir Classics, Theological Library,* and *Whittaker's Popular Library*. Of 437 titles (of which 96 had to be classified miscellaneous) there were 97 biographies (65 of individuals, 32 collective), outnumbering all other categories, including history (70), religion (84), travel (54), science (29), art (3), correspondence (3), and novels (1). This is perhaps as close to a Book-of-the-Month tabulation as can be made for the nineteenth century.

century's interest in popular taste and mass appeal, it should not be forgotten that this great popularity and production made possible or perhaps even necessitated a later emergence of aesthetic principles and recognition of biography as an art. And it should never be overlooked that, in spite of all the difficulties, there appeared many first-rate biographies of the second order, some flawed works of the first rank such as Moore's *Byron,* and at least two masterpieces in Southey's *Nelson* and Lockhart's *Scott.* The quality of the best of these exceeds that of any thirty-eight years of our own century.

To appreciate the quality of the heights, it is necessary to explore the depths. Two of the ruling passions of biography of the period grew out of concerns external to the art of biography: mass production and mass readership produced a concern for the new readers and their sensitive, unformed minds, which in turn brought about a resurgence of an old biographical bugaboo, the exemplary principle; and the extreme contemporaneity of biography led to concern for the subject's privacy, resulting in a new check, the doctrine of dignity. These are examined in the next two chapters.

CHAPTER TWO

BIOGRAPHY AS EXAMPLE

With the expansion and extension of life-writing, unknown writers might logically have been expected to turn to sensation and scandal, and to produce lives based on the careers of condemned criminals and theatrical personalities, on the pattern of eighteenth-century popular biography.

But this was the nineteenth century. Allan Cunningham gave a clue to the difference in his comparison of Johnson's *Lives* with Boswell's *Life:* "The chief fault of [Boswell's] . . . performance is, that it wants the splendid summary, and final judgment of character, which forms the crowning glory to the 'Lives of the Poets.' We are left to draw our own conclusions from the anecdotes and indications of Boswell, and the consequence is, that every one forms a mental character according to his abilities or prejudices, and nothing is fixed or defined."[1] The reading public had changed. Critics, publishers, and writers were conscious of the new readers and their impressionable minds. Literature could be of service to the unformed minds of these readers only if it was grounded in a firm foundation of morality which would give direction to its examples, a universal significance—and perhaps a moral—to its conclusions.

1. *Biographical and Critical History of the British Literature of the Last Fifty Years* (1834), pp. 244–45.

27

Publishers, writers, and critics were now in control of a mass medium, and such power for good must have a new conscience. The principles of the Evangelical movement apparently filled the bill.

The effect of the Evangelical movement was not felt all at once. Survey historians of biography seem to insist upon regarding the results of the Evangelical influence as a social symptom peculiar to the reign of Victoria. It is more productive, and far more realistic, to separate the artistic history of biography from identification with reigns and other literary movements. It is unsound, I think, to refer to the lives of this period as Romantic biography. As Garraty has pointed out,[2] the Romantic movement never really became an issue in biography: the Evangelical movement was already too firmly entrenched. And Victoria did not establish moral earnestness by royal decree. Earnestness was a growing mood, not a descending cloud.[3]

L. E. Elliott-Binns, in a thorough study of the Evangelical movement,[4] traces its beginnings to the first quarter of the eighteenth century, not neglecting its background in events of the seventeenth century. The influence of the movement upon literature had certainly been felt by the last quarter of the eighteenth century, and it was having its effect upon biography in the first years of the nineteenth century in a form which amounted to an Evangelical canon law of aesthetics. The *Annual Review,* not an Evangelical organ itself (at least not consciously so) was as early as 1802 espousing critical principles parallel to the party line of Evangelical aesthetics.

The office of the biographer, is indeed distinct from that of the moralist; and to estimate correctly the merit or demerit

2. Garraty, *The Nature of Biography* (1957), pp. 97, 98, 100, 101.

3. See Harold Nicolson, *The Development of English Biography* (1928), pp. 109–10. Stauffer (*I*, 311–23) suggests that a strong element of exemplary biography in the eighteenth century was growing weaker by the middle of the century. Its strength in the eighties and nineties undoubtedly marks the beginning of the resurgence of the exemplary principle in the nineteenth century.

4. *The Early Evangelicals* (1953), passim.

of each character, is obviously, from the number of circumstances to be taken into account, a very difficult task; yet surely, one who professes "to serve the interests of truth and virtue," scarcely performs her duty in omitting to embrace the opportunities of stigmatizing vice, when presented under the seductive garb of tenderness and sentiment. . . . Some of the anecdotes . . . [of this book] . . . however amusing in circumstance, and decorous in language, might have been sacrificed with advantage to the *sacred ignorance* and unpolluted purity of female youth, yet unknowing of the very existence of evil. A tendency to set talent above virtue, in the general estimate of character, and an opinion that strong passions are indicative of general abilities, we observed with concern.[5]

The *Annual Review* should not be identified with the cause of earnestness and suppression; its principles of criticism (at this time closely connected with Robert Southey's critical principles) are much too complex and diverse to be characterized by a single review. Yet some Evangelical ideals of aesthetics were absorbed, as if by osmosis, by a number of un-Evangelical or even anti-Evangelical critics. The Evangelical movement could not have changed the course of biography, or transformed its role by its members' writings alone. But the attitude it encouraged in biographers and the mission it recognized for biography were so pervasive that its cause was adopted by many who had no sympathy for religious enthusiasm.

The role which the Evangelicals assigned biography had its roots in an old (perhaps the oldest) aim of biography: to provide a literary memorial of the deceased, so that those who came after him might know his life, works, and character.

And as our country is intitled to its share of honour, in having produced many persons . . . whose memorable virtues, learning, and public labours have deserved to be transmitted to posterity; so it is some further credit to it, that justice has usually been done to their merits by the pens of their sur-

5. Review of Mary Hays' *Female Biography* (1802), *Annual Review, 1*, 612.

vivors, which, after the public have been deprived of their personal services, have kept their characters alive for . . . instruction and improvement, as well as entertainment.[6]

This is a laudable motive, shared (at least in part) by Plutarch, Cavendish, Walton, and Boswell. But the Evangelicals wrought a slight change upon it, sufficient to transform the whole meaning of the aim: memorial became example and character became virtue. He whose life provided an example most worthy of emulation best deserved the tribute of biography. Virtues dominated features which might better characterize a life. More than this: virtue was the essential, *qualifying* the individual for biographical treatment.

John Watkins, a biographer whose feet were always firmly planted in the eighteenth century, had no difficulty finding historical justification for biography's exemplary mission.

It was a custom with the antient Egyptians, when persons of eminence departed this life, to institute a minute investigation of their conduct in the midst of a general assembly of the people, and according as the balance was found to preponderate on the side of virtue, so was the degree of respect awarded by the public voice to their remains. After making all due allowance for ordinary errors, and unavoidable infirmities, if the character appeared worthy of general imitation, no honours were thought too great, or ceremonies too expensive, to endear the memory of the deceased, and to perpetuate the record of his actions. What was thus practiced by a nation proverbially celebrated for wisdom, is now become the province of the Historian; . . . it is his chronicle only that posterity will consult for the deeds of those who in their day were distinguished above the rest of mankind. Here, as in the grave, the mighty are on a level with the mean. . . . Nothing can kindle the emotion of gratitude, the sentiment of admiration, and the feeling of emulation, in contemplating the sepulchres of the great, but the faithful memorial of those

6. Thomas Sharp, *The Life of John Sharp* (1825), *1,* iii–iv.

virtues which will alone remain fragrant amidst the murkiness of the tomb.[7]

This could be one biographer's opinion, or a statement designed to emphasize the virtue of his subject. But it is repeated over and over again with the consistency of law and the conviction of doctrine. Presentation of the life as virtuous example became a prefatory formula almost as prevalent as the fictional safeguard, "any similarity to any persons living or dead." It was always "hoped" that the life might "contribute towards the formation of similar eminence; . . . inspire with noble endeavour . . . to the cause of truth and piety."[8]

Inherent in the rule of virtuous example was the corollary: it was a mistake to set talent above virtue.[9] Eminence in worldly affairs should not be considered qualification for biographical recognition after death. Dr. Johnson had sanctioned the writing of obscure men's lives, and the nineteenth century applied his sanction (stripped of its principles) with a vengeance. Since virtue was to be considered before talent and worldly eminence, simple accounts of homely but pious adequacy, which in the eighteenth century might have been circulated privately as family memorials, were now issued by commercial publishers and distributed by booksellers all over the kingdom. Thomas Sharp, in the preface to his *Life of John Sharp,* admits that he set out to provide a volume of extracts from John Sharp's private journal, for private family circulation ("a *most instructive lesson* to the Archbishop's grandchildren"). But in the execution of "this as yet narrow design, so many things offered themselves for enlarging it . . . viz. the *principles* by which he conducted himself in all parts of life, the inviolable *integrity* that regulated and reigned in all he said or did, and the noble *simplicity* which

7. John Watkins, *Memoirs of Her . . . Majesty, Sophia-Charlotte* (2 vols. 1819), *1,* v–vi. For two eighteenth-century antecedents of this theme (1740 and 1788), cf. Stauffer, *1,* 496 and 549–50.

8. Quoted from the preface to Joseph Gilbert's *Memoir of the Life . . . of . . . Edward Williams* (1825), p. vi, but the words and phrases turn up in hundreds of other prefaces and advertisements.

9. See *Annual Review* quotation above, p. 29.

shone in his whole conversation and deportment,"[1] that the editor-compiler could not forbear its publication by Rivington and Company in two volumes octavo.

The Evangelicals, of course, did not meet to vote approval of biography as a moral art; they did not recommend a specific approach to biographers or threaten publishers with boycott for their part in the production of unexemplary lives. In our era of motivational research and subliminal persuasion, it is difficult to conceive of a popular movement which was, in the strictest sense of the word, popular. We cannot believe that a disorganized, unplanned, unsystematically executed program of public persuasion could accomplish its aims so well, or so profoundly influence a mode of literary expression.

In an oversimplified view of the movement, it can be said that the Evangelicals saw in biography a kind of popular reading virtually made for their purposes. Did not the Gospels demonstrate the propriety and prove the efficacy of biography? Few of them would have thought of the example of the medieval Church, but had not hagiography there again proved the point? Reviewers in the periodicals continually reminded them of the appeal which memoirs and lives shared with novels[2]: the appeal of uncomplicated narrative, most potent among the ranks of new readers.

Certain highly objectionable elements that had become identified with biographical writing would of course have to be

1. *Life of John Sharp* (1825), *I*, iv–v.
2. The reminders were not universally enthusiastic about biography's popularity, to say the least. "The desultory, defective, and often erroneous and inconsistent intelligence conveyed in . . . [periodical] publications, constitutes half the stock of knowledge of a considerable portion of the reading world . . . and novels, books of travels, and memoirs, make up the remainder. . . . We own we are astonished that books of this sort should continue to be read with such avidity. . . . Some of the memoirs that have been lately published are highly valuable both in point of substance and composition, but the greater part of them are little superior to novels on the score of authenticity, and inferior to them in every other quality" (review of *On the Rise, Progress, and Present State of Public Opinion, in Great Britain,* 1828, and two other works, *Quarterly Review, 39,* 497).

purged: the murder and mayhem of criminal lives, the glamor and excitement of theatrical lives, and plain unmitigated scandal—in short, all the elements which attracted "low curiosity." If biography were reserved as a tribute to those lives which merited virtue and emulation, however, even curiosity might be reformed. Once the public recognized this basic principle, and all biography was dedicated to the narration of virtue, low curiosity for scandal, crime, and gossip would wither and disappear, deprived of its opportunities for delectation.

They who look for particulars of regal pageantry will be little gratified in the perusal of this narrative; and still less will those readers be pleased whose vitiated taste is only to be allured by the whisperings of scandal, details of conversations that never occurred, and anecdotes of circumstances that originate only in the fertility of imagination. But happily there are minds who rise above the impertinence of idle curiosity, who seek information respecting departed excellence, not for amusement only, but for edification; and who, with an emulative spirit, wish to retrace the graces, which eminently adorned a long life of usefulness, that they may be enabled, as far as the difference of station will permit, to "go and do likewise." [3]

And the moral effect of exemplary biography would not end with simple emulation: this was but the first link of a chain of actions which (it was conceived) would spread morality across the nation with inexorable speed and efficiency. Biography became a part of the nineteenth century's great mission for itself as a bridge to the future.

There is a double office served by [memoirs and biographies].
. . . If [the subject] has been intellectually or morally eminent, his life creates something . . . corresponding . . .—the strong hold upon our admiration and sympathies, begets a kindred style of character. If his eminence be of an opposite order, a

3. John Watkins, *Memoirs of . . . Sophia-Charlotte* (1819), *1*, vii–viii.

true portraiture sets up, in the height of our astonishment, a warning beacon, of perhaps almost equal value. Memoirs and biographies have another tendency; they beget in the living, a desire to merit posthumous respect and honour, like that which is paid by us to our celebrated ancestors. There is thus and therefore a continually enlarging host of witnesses gathering around every succeeding generation, whose examples, admonitions, and warnings, may be expected to make every new race wiser and better than its predecessors.[4]

A worldly system of rewards after death was set up on a circular plan; a place in history, by means of a published biography, was held out to those who profited well by their reading and successfully emulated the examples set forth in the virtuous lives of others. Example begat emulation, which begat virtue, which begat biography. Worldly immortality was now within the reach of all who demonstrated virtue, regardless of talent or fame, and to all who read carefully and imitated well. The bridge to the future was paved with exemplary biographies.

The eagerness to qualify for emulation produced the extreme manifestations of piety for which the nineteenth century is so justly noted.

In speaking of the lives of eminent men, it may admit of a question, whether those that have been short, or those that have been lengthened to the utmost verge allotted to our race, be the most instructive. We certainly think nothing can be more impressive than the death of a young man. To be cut off in the vigour of life and ere it has been ripened, is the most arresting and appalling of events. But when the life, though short, has been lovely, that is, when it has been well occupied with the duties open to its possessor, there is a solemn attraction in an early death, that makes the living look upon it, as an event worthy of imitative reparation.[5]

4. Review of Alonzo King's *Memoirs of George Dana Boardman* (1834), *Monthly Review*, IV, *14*, 367–68.
5. Ibid.

The literature of these short but lovely lives and young but happy deaths is repugnant. Deathbed scenes were anthologized;[6] children, dead at the age of seven, ten, or fifteen, were celebrated with biographical tributes complete with letters and literary productions (for the most part sermons and meditations).[7] To us these are extreme and ludicrous misuses of biography—calling to mind nothing so much as Huck Finn's encounter with the spirit of Emmeline Grangerford.[8] But if (as the Evangelical canon of biography held) the short, happy life without taint of evil is more uplifting than the long, profitable life, these were the perfect subjects for exemplary biography.[9]

Had the influence of the exemplary principle been limited

6. William Wilberforce and his followers seem to have collected and exchanged accounts of happy deathbeds with the avidity usually shown only by small boys for bubble-gum cards. Published compendia of such scenes and sayings include Henry Clissold's *The Last Hours of Eminent Christians, from the Commencement of the Christian Era to the Death of George the Third* (1829), 552 pp.; Ingram Cobbin's *Dying Sayings of Eminent Christians* (1828); *Scenes of Death* by J. Thwaites, M.D. (1837); and John Warton's [i.e. William Wood's] *Death-bed Scenes and Pastoral Conversations* (3 vols. 1827).

7. Anthologies of such brief brief lives were also popular: *The Nursery Plutarch* (1833); *Anecdotes, and Dying Testimonies of Young Persons, Especially Sunday Scholars* (1828); *Early Blossoms . . . Biographical Notices of Individuals Distinguished by Their Genius and Attainment, Who Died in Their Youth* (1819).

8. The message of most of these is brilliantly summed up in Huck's analysis: "If Emmeline Grangerford could make poetry like that before she was fourteen, there ain't no telling what she could 'a' done by and by" (chapter 17).

9. The effect of such publications on the youth which they proposed to uplift seems to have misfired on occasion. The *Monthly Review* cites a quotation from Mrs. E. Whitty's *A Mother's Journal during the Last Illness of Her Daughter, Sarah Chisman* (1820) as the strongest possible objection to publishing youthful religious biography: " 'When I was quite a little child, I used to read the accounts of the deaths of good children, and think that when I came to die, *I would use the same expressions which they did:* —I never thought, Mamma, of *being* like them, which was all I *ought* to have thought of, you know' " (*Monthly Review*, II, *94*, 224; quotation from p. 103 of the work).

to such grotesques, it would not be of much concern, but the principle was pervasive and surprisingly adaptable. Even biographers of artists and men of letters (one might expect them, at least, to constitute the opposition) took up the pattern of example, though they could not provide the piety. Intellectual or artistic growth replaced piety and virtue.

Where moderate wealth and superficial education are so widely diffused as in these Islands, it is natural that a great number of persons should betake themselves to reading merely to relieve the tediousness of mental vacancy and inaction, and . . . have recourse to books that merely excite, . . . without harrassing them with the toil of thinking. Hence histories of private and domestic life, whether real or fictitious, whether in the form of biography or novels, become the most popular, and consequently the most lucrative and abundant species of writing; till, by continually pampering and satiating, without at all contributing to feed, nourish, or invigorate public taste, they completely vitiate and enervate it. . . . From this charge, however, the histories of those lives, which have been successfully devoted to the cultivation and improvement of the useful and elegant arts, should be most honourably exempted: since it is chiefly by being made acquainted by the details of their progress, the method of their studies, and the means of their acquirements, together with the adventitious aids which accelerated, or the obstacles which impeded them, that others are enabled to arrive at the same end, by a nearer and more direct road; and to extend the benefits of improvement and discovery still farther.[1]

The critic comes to attack contemporary biography, but stays to endorse the exemplary principle, in part responsible for the shortcomings of biography which he sets out to criticize.

If the subject's virtue commended him to biographical treatment, the greater the virtue, the greater the respect the book commanded. The measure of quality was the subject's moral

1. Review of James Northcote's *Memoirs of Sir Joshua Reynolds* (1813), *Edinburgh Review*, 23, 263–64.

beauty, not the biographer's artistic skill. The biographer was only the organizer and compiler of documents. He made certain that the virtues were properly displayed in order, that vices (wherever present) were properly stigmatized. The subject was the real artist, acting out the virtuous progress, battling an adverse environment, holding the good thought. The biographer was amanuensis to this artist of life and saw to it that his words and the incidents of his life were extracted, connected, and seen through the press. He deserved a measure of respect and public gratitude for his selfless labors, but contemporary critics tended to ignore his selective, stylistic, and dramatic efforts. Too true that to ignore artistry was to deal most kindly with most of these books: too many amateurs had been attracted to biography by the apparent simplicity of the form, and too many lives were being farmed out by publishers to willing and unskilled hands. But the sensibility which reduced the biographer to the status of copyist encouraged little development in the art and would have failed to recognize development when it appeared on its own.

CHAPTER THREE

DIGNITY AND SUPPRESSION

Biographical suppression—the omission of authentic documents, or portions of documents, and the deliberate misrepresentation of facts—has too often been ascribed to Victorian prudery or to puritanical self-censorship of vice, or, indeed, of any sexual activity. If suppression is to be appreciated as a natural outgrowth of biography's development rather than as just another element of Victorian social history, a more realistic estimate of its origins and a more temperate consideration of the arguments in favor of suppression are needed. The nature of the information withheld and the principles which dictated suppression are much too complex to be dismissed as prudery, puritanism, or propriety.

When Thomas Moore, sitting at his table, suspended his transcription and omitted a passage of a Byron letter to insert a string of his famous asterisks, he was motivated by a complex of personal judgments, not by a principle of suppression. He suppressed what he thought the public, his publishers, Byron's relatives and friends, or posterity would not stand for or what he wanted cut—not those passages that conflicted with a doctrine of nineteenth-century biography. The study of literary history, however, cannot dismiss any antiliterary phenomenon as "a sign of the times." It would be presumptuous of us to atomize and particularize the principles within any nineteenth-century mind, but it is necessary to define the principles themselves if we are to explain some of the wildly illogical manifestations of suppression in the early nineteenth century.

The application of the exemplary principle led to suppression that was, for the most part, more an act of omission than commission. Exemplary deeds, thoughts, and writings were selected from the jumbled mass of vacillating and diversely motivated impulses, decisions, and actions which made up the subject's life. Clarity, unity, and virtuous example were gained at the expense of candor, humanity, and true biography. Such selectivity can be confused with the concern for the security of personal privacy prevalent at the time. This was the rebirth of an eighteenth-century doctrine of biographical dignity, every bit as damaging to the cause of candid and true biography as the exemplary principle, and far more difficult to understand.

Historians of the eighteenth century had espoused a doctrine of selectivity in writing history which became known as the "dignity of history." J. B. Black ascribes the doctrine to William Robertson.

> What he meant by the phrase was not merely that history should be written in a dignified manner, but principally that it should be written about dignified events and characters. In a sense . . . it is simply a variant of the maxims laid down by Voltaire and Hume regarding the selection of *data*. . . . It tended to rule out many facts, altogether as too trivial to be noticed by history, to skim lightly over others as more or less negligible, and to concentrate almost entirely on those transactions which necessarily demand attention because of their inherent interest, or because of the instruction to be derived from them. . . . The doctrine . . . encourages the historian to look askance on circumstantial detail as matter of inferior grade and texture, and to suppress it wherever possible.[1]

The doctrine of dignity was less well defined for biography, and was clearly motivated by considerations of personal privacy. In

1. *The Art of History* (1926), pp. 131–33.

other words, it arose out of a concern for the subject, not from a concern for the literary product. Stauffer indicates that Addison was the "most powerful champion of discreet biography,"[2] but the quotation he cites by Abel Boyer best represents the doctrine as it was to reappear in the nineteenth century: "My design is to represent and record his publick, not his private Life; and to avoid what I ever accounted a Fault in Biographers, the raking into minute Domestick Passages, exposing Privacies to publick View."[3]

Later in the century, Dr. Johnson attacked the ideal of dignified distance and generality,[4] and anecdotists and intimate biographers did much to break it down. According to Stauffer, neither Addison's "cold and formal ideal" nor the "sordid practice" of the booksellers prevailed. "Writers [of biography] came to believe that absolute truthfulness was essential and that this could be secured only by the preservation and inclusion of exact, minute, personal detail."[5]

It might be expected that Boswell's *Life of Johnson* would have dealt the death-blow to the doctrine of biographical dignity once for all. It introduced a variety of personal meditations and private conversations, violated the confidence of epistolary correspondence, and depicted its subject in bad moods as well as good. Everything which set forth Johnson in a new light or enforced one of Boswell's previous points, regardless of dignity or decorum, found a place in the *Life,* provided only that it did not conflict with the biographer's mental image of his subject. He transferred all responsibility for the dignity of his work to this image: if it was correct, truthful, and complete, any detail

2. The passage he cites to support this assertion is from *The Freeholder,* no. 35, 20 April 1716 (Stauffer, *1,* 530–31).

3. *Memoirs of the Life and Negotiations of Sir W. Temple* (1714), p. 418, quoted by Stauffer, *1,* 530.

4. To an assertion by Boswell that he feared he had recorded "too many little incidents," Johnson replied "There is nothing, Sir, too little for so little a creature as man. It is by studying little things that we attain the great art of having as little misery and as much happiness as possible" (*Life of Johnson,* ed. Hill-Powell, 1934, *1,* 433, 14 July 1763).

5. Stauffer, *1,* 535–36.

which enhanced, supported, or illustrated it would have the dignity of his subject's living presence.

Boswell might well have killed off the doctrine of dignified distance if his book had been understood. As it was, however, the *Life* and its portrait of Johnson were praised, but critics and men of letters found Boswell's methods crude and questioned the dignity of his "particulars."[6] They viewed with alarm the precedent set (or rather the precedents broken) by his methods. The doctrine of dignity was reborn.

Coleridge sounded the keynote of the new doctrine in *The Friend.*

> An inquisitiveness into the minutest circumstances and casual sayings of eminent contemporaries, is indeed quite natural; but so are all our follies, and the more natural they are, the more caution should we exert in guarding against them. To scribble Trifles even on the perishable glass of an Inn window, is the mark of an Idler; but to engrave them on the Marble Monument, sacred to the memory of the departed Great, is something worse than Idleness. The spirit of genuine Biography is in nothing more conspicuous, than in the firmness with which it withstands the cravings of worthless curiosity, as distinguished from the thirst after useful knowledge.[7]

William Wordsworth, writing to James Gray in response to a review of a life of Burns which Gray had sent him, expounded the new doctrine most systematically. He found the primary tenet in the gentleman's regard for every man's right to privacy.

> Only to philosophy enlightened by the affections does it belong justly to estimate the claims of the deceased on the one hand, and of the present age and future generations, on the other; and to strike a balance between them.—Such philosophy runs a risk of becoming extinct among us, if the coarse intrusions into the recesses, the gross breaches upon the sanc-

6. See above, Chapter One, pp. 10–11, for H. N. Coleridge's views on this.
7. "A Prefatory Observation on Modern Biography," no. 21, 25 Jan. 1810, *The Friend,* p. 338.

tities, of domestic life, to which we have lately been more and more accustomed, are to be regarded as indications of a vigorous state of public feeling favourable to the maintenance of the liberties of our country.—Intelligent lovers of freedom are from necessity bold and hardy lovers of truth; but, according to the measure in which their love is intelligent, is it attended with a finer discrimination, and a more sensitive delicacy. The wise and good . . . respect, as one of the noblest characteristics of Englishmen, that jealousy of familiar approach, which . . . is one of the most efficacious guardians of rational public freedom.[8]

He then articulated specific rights to enforce this basic respect: for the living, due regard for their personal or domestic privacy; for the dead, respect for the national reputation or public character they had earned during life. These rights he further enforced by a series of rules for the use of specific biographical materials. The subject's letters to his friends were intended for their eyes alone, his journals and memoranda for his own eyes. His recorded prayers and meditations were perhaps most sacred, bearing the divine seal of man's communication with God.

As with the exemplary principle, the law was nowhere enacted but everywhere observed. John Wilson Croker, the editor of Boswell, was not a fully convinced proponent of the doctrine, but he did support one principle. He attacked the sons of William Wilberforce in the *Quarterly* for violating a primary privacy: every man had an inviolable right to designate what he wanted published.

They tell us that these memoranda "bear upon them an order for their destruction, which it was only within the last years of his life that he so far recalled as to desire them to be submitted with his other papers to the judgment of his nearest relatives. *Perhaps he was himself scarcely aware of the value of the documents which he was thus laying open. . . .* When,

8. "Letter to a Friend of Burns" (1816), reprinted in *Wordsworth's Literary Criticism,* ed. Nowell C. Smith (1905), p. 210.

on Mr. Wilberforce's decease, these stores were unexpectedly committed to the writers, their first feeling was an unwillingness to *expose to the public gaze what was so plainly of a confidential character.* 'A life which is worth reading,' was the pointed saying of Mackintosh, 'ought never to have been written.' But there are some characters fitted to exert so permanent an influence, and so clearly marked as examples to mankind that in their case private delicacy yields to public good. Whether the present is one of these excepted instances, the *readers* of the following work *must decide."—Preface,* pp. vi., vii. [italics Croker's] Before we can come to the decision which we are thus . . . invited to make, we should require a clearer explanation of some important points: . . . such as *how far,* and with *what design,* Mr. Wilberforce departed from his first intention. . . . If Mr. Wilberforce did . . . revoke the order for the destruction of these papers, he may have done so in the expectation that they might interest and edify the survivors of his own family circle, but without any idea of general publication: nay, he may have contemplated the possibility of their being *consulted* by some future biographer for dates and facts, without sanctioning their being "exposed" *in extenso* "to the public gaze" so soon after his death, and while so many of those mentioned—often unfavourably— were still living, to feel with the deeper pain even the slightest censure from one so loved and honoured. . . . The publication will not, we think, add much to Mr. Wilberforce's reputation as a public man—nothing, certainly, to the popular estimate of his talents—and, strange to say, not much even to his personal history. . . . The reason of this unexpected insipidity appears clearly enough. . . . Mr. Wilberforce's notes were *bonâ fide* memoranda—mere helps to his own memory—. . . obscure from their brevity . . . generally confined to little personal matters of very feeble interest. We do not suppose there ever before was so large a mass of notes which tell so little even about the writer himself.[9]

9. Review of *The Life of William Wilberforce* (1838), *Quarterly Review,* 62, 215–17.

As publishers scraped around for new material, memorabilia and juvenilia were brought out separately or used to fatten up prospective titles. Reviewers reasserted respect for author's wishes not for the sake of principle alone, but in order to stem what many of them regarded as "trash" or "useless publication."[1]

It does not follow, because a man in the course of his life has produced works of sterling merit, that every juvenile performance or hasty sketch is therefore interesting. . . . The fragments of a work of Milton could never be uninteresting, and the desultory speculations of a Newton might lead to some important discovery: but Miltons and Newtons are rare productions.[2]

Undeniably, some of the "trash" the periodical critics continually protested against *was* trash. But the objections contained within them the seeds of a law of biographical distance harmless enough in principle but undeniably dangerous in extreme application. Too particular a concern for author's wishes

1. "It is certainly desirable that memoirs of eminent and exemplary persons should be written, but it is by no means desirable or necessary, that they should all be written in quarto. Those of Mrs. Carter, whose life was singularly barren of incident, might have been comprised in a moderate octavo, with manifest advantage to all . . . concerned, except perhaps the editor. In that case, early poems, of which in maturer years their author was ashamed, would not have been disrespectfully dragged back to notice, . . . slight and imperfect notes, written in the margin of her bible, evidently without a thought beyond her private use, would never have swelled out a pompous title-page; and we should not have found it our duty, to preface this . . . with a reprimand to 'her nephew and executor' " (review of Montagu Pennington's *Memoirs of the Life of Mrs. Elizabeth Carter,* 1807, *Annual Review,* 6, 386–87).

2. Review of J. Wooll's *Biographical Memoirs of the late Dr. Joseph Warton* (1806), *Annual Review,* 5, 299. Samuel Johnson evidently did not measure up to the standard of merit required to render minor writings worthy of publication. An *Account of the Life of Doctor Samuel Johnson, from His Birth to His Eleventh Year,* published in 1805, was almost universally attacked as insignificant. "This volume was among the mass of papers which Dr. Johnson ordered to be committed to the flames a few days before his death: the Doctor's black servant saved them, and the editor

leads to incomplete biographical accounts and undocumented lives. Twentieth-century biographers of Matthew Arnold are still thwarted by his wishes and his family's almost fanatic regard for them, a survival of this early nineteenth-century doctrine. In other instances, it is not unlikely that surviving members of a family, finding the "author's wishes" their best defense, might have manufactured some desires for the dead.

Extreme application of principle was, of course, a nineteenth-century specialty. "Author's wishes" was only a point of departure for a system of discretionary rules set forth in Thomas Sharp's *Life of John Sharp.*

> One thing . . . is manifest, that [the journal] was solely calculated for his own private and particular use: and, therefore, in selecting passages . . . in subserviency to another design, and that of a public nature too, some care and discretion was to be used. . . . He abominated scandal, and giving of characters, as much as any man alive, and was always wont . . . to speak very warily and tenderly of every thing that touched another's credit and reputation. . . . The rule, then, which was laid down and pursued, with respect to the choice or suppression of what the diary afforded, was this: to extract from thence no more than was apparently conducive to one or other of these ends, viz. either to the *connecting* some parts of this life together, and adjusting the series . . . in proper order of time; or to the clearing up and explaining the more remarkable matters of fact that occur in this account; or to

---

purchased them from his widow! In this disgraceful manner are these insignificant papers brought before the public eye, and puffed in a pompous preface as relics of great curiosity and interest. We are sorry to see such flagrant impositions on the public attempted, and feel it a duty to counteract the success of them as well as we can" (*Annual Review* for 1805, *4*, 484). The difference between our present attitude and that of the contemporary reviewer is apparent when we consider that the manuscript of this particular account by Johnson has since disappeared, and our knowledge of the account is based upon this publication. Twentieth-century Johnsonians have reason to be grateful for this publication, a "flagrant imposition" to contemporaries.

the proving and confirming what is said of his sentiments and principles in politics; or to the giving him his just and true character in all parts of life, and *disproving whatever hath been falsely reported of him,* either by those who knew him not, or those who would not judge the most favourably of him, through the prejudice of party. . . . And further than this, no man has a right to make use of the MS. Diary, whatever property he may claim in the possession of it.[3]

The biographer could be trusted to draw discreet conclusions from the random, extemporary thoughts recorded in journals and diaries. The reader could not. No one so distrusted the common reader's independent interpretation as did the early nineteenth century. This is the major reason Boswell's book was regarded with such mixed feelings.[4]

If journals were dangerous, letters were doubly so. They violated the privacy of both sender and receiver. The reputation they had enjoyed as touchstones of the deepest emotions and most basic character was, Wordsworth felt, greatly overrated.

We have the author's letters discharged upon us in showers; but how few readers will take the trouble of comparing those letters with each other, and with the other documents of the publication, in order to come at a genuine knowledge of the

3. *Life of Sharp, 1,* xiii–xvi.

4. Twentieth-century biography has realized the potential of many of the nineteenth century's in extenso publications of journals and memoranda. The much-criticized Wilberforce memoirs have been highly useful to both biographers and historians of the Evangelical movement (e.g. L. E. Elliott-Binns, *The Early Evangelicals,* 1953). Our smug hindsight should not prejudice our understanding of the early nineteenth century's impatience with undigested journals. Whether we like it or not, the more systematic knowledge of psychology makes our reading of personal revelations of this sort very different from that of the average, or even the exceptional nineteenth-century reader. We certainly read Boswell's *Johnson* differently. To them (as Croker demonstrated, almost too well) the book was a source of knowledge of history, men, and manners. They overlooked the delights to be found in a study of its subject, its narrator, and its lesser characters. It was appreciated perhaps as much then, but for different reasons.

writer's character!—The life of Johnson by Boswell had broken through many pre-existing delicacies, and afforded the British public an opportunity of acquiring experience, which before it had happily wanted; nevertheless, at the time when the ill-selected medley of Burns's correspondence first appeared, little progress had been made (nor is it likely that, by the mass of mankind, much ever will be made) in determining what portion of these confidential communications escapes the pen in courteous, yet often innocent, compliance—to gratify the several tastes of correspondents; and as little towards distinguishing opinions and sentiments uttered for the momentary amusement merely of the writer's own fancy, from those which his judgment deliberately approves, and his heart faithfully cherishes.[5]

Even less conservative critics, who held that letters represented the sincere feelings of the writer, felt that publication of letters should be undertaken only with great caution. The *Annual Review's* general article on biography and correspondence for 1805 reflected this growing concern.

The modern fashion of writing biography, is to render the person celebrated as much as possible his own historian, by the publication of his private correspondence; a method which, although possessed of some peculiar advantages, is at the same time liable to many objections. In the first place it is a strong inducement to misjudging or unprincipled persons to violate the confidence of epistolary correspondence, and publish to the world the unguarded and unpremeditated effusions of friendship; in consequence of which, the literary, and even moral, character of the writer may be unjustly, yet plausibly, brought into jeopardy; and much uneasiness may be given to persons incidentally mentioned or alluded to. It is also pampering a base appetite for private scandal and anecdote, and for an impertinent inquisitiveness into circumstances which strangers have no right to know.[6]

5. *Wordsworth's Literary Criticism*, pp. 207–08.
6. *Annual Review* (for 1804), *3*, 470.

Repeated mention of the "base appetite for private scandal" and "an impertinent inquisitiveness" throughout this period demonstrates how acutely the pressure of contemporaneous publication was felt.

There is an artistic myopia here. The nineteenth-century biographer was expected to exercise selectivity, but a selectivity motivated by propriety, not by the aims of literary art. He was recommended to his task not by his artistic skill or vision but by his high regard for personal privacy. A reviewer for the *Monthly*, describing the rather confused situation which surrounded the assignment of a biographer to the life of Sir Thomas Lawrence, emphasizes the quality of discretion above all others.

> The name of the poet was put forward on the occasion, merely for the purpose of deterring from the destined prey, the minor vagrants of the forest. It might serve, moreover, to attract communications from relatives and friends, who would have no difficulty in confiding to the discretion of so respectable a man, papers of a confidential nature, from which useful information might be extracted, without wounding the delicacies of family privacy, or exposing more than the world had a justifiable interest in knowing.[7]

The "minor vagrants" could not be trusted. The poet, surprisingly enough, could be counted upon to act with the utmost delicacy.

Even in the matter of spiritual diaries and intimate religious testaments, where there could be no danger of scandal, no possibility of the "giving of character," there seems to have been a definite feeling that the strictest safeguards of privacy should be invoked. That the inviolability of religious meditations was an article of the doctrine of dignity is the strongest

7. Review of D. E. Williams' *Life and Correspondence of Sir Thomas Lawrence* . . . (1831), in *Monthly Review*, IV, 2, 244. It was announced that Thomas Campbell was gathering materials for a life of Lawrence, but he actually did next to nothing in preparation or composition. See Williams' Preface to *Life and Correspondence*.

indication that the doctrine survived from the eighteenth century, and was not a product of the Evangelical movement's exemplary principle. On this particular point, in fact, the exemplary principle and the doctrine of dignity met head-on. Adherents of dignity felt that publication of intimate details of piety violated privacy as surely as intimate details of vice. Publication of prayers and meditations was just another relaxation of the safeguards of personal privacy, another symptom of the collapse of the gentleman's discretion. Such a feeling was current early in the century, but by the 1830s reviews indicate that, with more and more pious lives, the inclusion of prayers and meditations and spiritual progresses had proved themselves so valuable in the service of exemplary biography that their "utility" far outweighed any considerations of privacy. John Wilson Croker favored the inclusion of such "solemn communings of a soul with its Saviour."

> We agree that as a frequent practice it would be full of danger, and that the instances in which such a publication could be creditable to the dead, or profitable to the living, must be extremely rare. . . . The evil of the abuse may be great; but still greater is the good which may be produced by the practical example of a high religious influence predominating over all human passions in men eminent for talents, station, and brilliancy in society, or for activity and intelligence in the business of the world. It is of vast importance to convince the ordinary run of mankind . . . that a deep religious feeling is . . . the best auxiliary to the successful exercise of the ordinary duties and the attainment of the highest honours of human society.[8]

His review went on to regret the lack of such revelations in Burke's biography, and to cite the contribution which the publication of Johnson's *Prayers and Meditations* had made to public welfare and morals "by affording to feeble minds

8. Review of the Wilberforces' *Life of William Wilberforce* (1838), in *Quarterly Review*, 62, 218.

the consolatory and encouraging example, that an intellect so powerful . . . was yet humble before God."[9]

When they ventured beyond rules for the use of specific biographic materials, adherents of biographical dignity were less precise in their requirements but more insistent upon their principles. First, they felt that the "fame" and "reputation" of the subject and the feelings of his family were to be considered. In the most conservative interpretation of this rather vague concept, nothing, not even the truth, should be written of the subject's blood-relatives which might "give them pain" directly, and nothing should be written of the deceased which, by injuring his fame, might injure them indirectly. Wordsworth again espoused the narrow view.

> Silence is a privilege of the grave, a right of the departed: let him, therefore, who infringes that right . . . take heed that he opens not his mouth without a sufficient sanction. De mortuis nil nisi bonum, is a rule in which these sentiments have been pushed to an extreme that proves how deeply humanity is interested in maintaining them. . . . Penalties of law, conventions of manners, and personal fear, protect the reputation of the living; and something of this protection is extended to the recently dead,—who survive, to a certain degree, in their kindred and friends.[1]

It is a hard rule, if conservatively applied. *De mortuis nil nisi bonum* is very nearly the most effective preventive of good biography, and a natural tonic for panegyric and hagiography.

9. Ibid., p. 218. Thomas Sharp had considered suppressing religious memoranda from his *Life of John Sharp,* and relented for similar reasons. "It may seem, indeed, *to be a question,* how far it is honourable or respectful to his memory, not to suppress totally . . . his private devotions and communication with God. . . . To have done thus, purely to gratify the curiosity of men, or to enlarge the history, had not been so easily pardonable, yet, when it is done with a view to the real benefit of all who shall peruse it, as a probable means of making them better, the candid and serious reader will scarcely censure it as a fault" (*Life of Sharp, 1,* xvi).

1. *Wordsworth's Literary Criticism,* pp. 209–10.

As applied to the subject himself, this rule would suppress any materials or observations from his own mouth which showed him acting from any motivations lower than those which characterized the high points or chief virtues of his character. It would suppress any incidents which reflected upon his character in a manner inconsistent with his eventual reputation. To say the least, such suppression would exert a stabilizing influence on reputation, but its effect on biography would be stultifying. Suppose the virtuous man had been a wayward youth: the matter was no longer relevant, since he had gone on to better things. Youthful misbehavior could not illustrate the man he became, but could only satisfy "low curiosity," or "lower his fame." This feature of the theory was honored by many critics less conservative than Wordsworth. Southey's review of William Hayley's *Life of Cowper* pointed out that the subject's early life—involved as it was with family principles, circumstances, and (in some instances) family cruelty—was an extremely delicate area.

> Curiosity was powerfully awakened to the history of such a man; and . . . it was imperfectly gratified during his life. . . . Every one was apprised that various reasons of delicacy existed, which might prohibit an undisguised narrative of all that concerned him; but it was hoped, that enough of the veil might be drawn aside, to exhibit the true features of his singular character, and the principal circumstances by which it was formed.[2]

Southey does not expect, or perhaps does not even desire, the "veil" to be removed completely.[3]

2. *Annual Review* (for 1803), 2, 457.

3. One writer, working as editor for an autobiography of a living subject, apparently felt pressures of family discretion which did not affect the subject himself. The editor was obliged to rein in the enthusiasm and candor of the autobiographer, suppressing a few of his more vivid memories. "The only difficulty I have had with him was in softening down the circumstances of his family concerns. I refused to go on with his life if he persisted in publishing all he had written down. I would not have given what is

Wordsworth's chief objection to Currie's *Life of Burns* hung on this tenuous question of "fame" and "reputation."

> If . . . it were in the power of a biographer to relate the truth, the *whole* truth, and nothing *but* the truth, the friends and surviving kindred of the deceased, for the sake of general benefit to mankind, might endure that such heart-rending communication should be made to the world. But in no case is this possible; and, in the present, the opportunities of directly acquiring other than superficial knowledge have been most scanty, . . . and to what purpose relate them even were they true, if the narrative cannot be heard without extreme pain; unless they are placed in such a light, and brought forward in such order, that they shall explain their own laws, and leave the reader in as little uncertainty as the mysteries of our nature will allow, respecting the spirit from which they derived their existence, and which governed the agent?[4]

Wordsworth's opinion of the efficacy of biography is clear. Since it is impossible for any life to capture the spirit which activated all the strengths and "infirmities" of any particular human character, no "infirmities" or shortcomings should be set forth. Since the "whole truth" is not obtainable in biography, the biographer should limit himself to instances which illustrate the highest reaches of the virtue, talent, and intellect of the subject. If the biographer can't say something good, he had better say nothing at all.

The rules of the doctrine of dignity were not published as such. The debate on dignity and privacy was not conducted in any formalized manner. The question of inclusion of religious

---

published, had I not thought it necessary to illustrate the effects that early education produces upon the after man, and at the same time to account for his bad success in life" (*The Life of Alexander Alexander: Written by Himself*, ed. John Howell, 1830, preface by Howell, pp. vi–vii).

4. *Wordsworth's Literary Criticism*, p. 205.

meditations demonstrates that the principles of dignity were neither so pervasive nor so powerful as those of exemplary biography. Yet the doctrine was highly significant in the formation of biographers' attitudes, particularly in the matter of the use of the personal documents. Beginning as a check on "low curiosity," the doctrine of dignity ended as a carefully articulated formula for "the suppression of profitable truth." Advocating the proper use of personal documents, it provided a sanction for the misuse of documentary biographical evidence. This in turn produced some of the editorial license which characterizes so much of nineteenth-century biography.

Two biographical situations arose in this period which demonstrate the practical workings of the forces of example and dignity: the publication of Lord Nelson's letters to Lady Hamilton, and the destruction of Lord Byron's memoirs. The two incidents pose different questions in the general area of dignity and suppression, but the public furor in the first instance and the private furor in the second arose from similar issues. The first involved the revelation of the private life of a public hero; the second, the public revelation of a private family squabble. In both, the "characters" given of contemporaries was a central issue. In the first, publication raised the storm, and in the second, suppression and destruction closed the question.

Horatio, Viscount Nelson, one of the most popular English heroes of modern times, was killed at Trafalgar 21 October 1805. Before the end of the year seven hastily concocted lives appeared; over the next five years, seventeen more, of varying degrees of completeness and originality, were published, ranging in scope from pamphlets of less than fifty pages to the massive *Life* by James Stanier Clarke and John M'Arthur, running to two volumes quarto.

In 1814, James Harrison, a hack whom Lady Hamilton had cultivated (and who had previously compiled a life of Nelson designed to gain her the pension she never received),[5] stole the

5. *The Life of the Right Honourable Horatio Lord Viscount Nelson* (2 vols. 1806); see Carola Oman, *Nelson* (1947), pp. vi–vii.

personal correspondence of Nelson and Lady Hamilton and sold it to Thomas Lovewell, who forthwith published it.[6] The publication was the final blow to Lady Hamilton's hopes for financial assistance, but the reviewers and the public nevertheless assumed that she had sold them herself, an opinion which added some fuel to the flames of righteous indignation.

The suspicion that Lady Hamilton was involved in the publication made it inevitable that the letters would be grouped with works designed to excite "low curiosity." The outrage at the revelations of the correspondence was aggravated by the idea that a woman could be guilty of "turning a penny" by exposing to public view intimate details of her own life. The major objection of the reviewers (those who even deigned to comment in periodicals upon such a scandalous publication) was not the charge of bookmaking or public exhibitionism, but rather that a truth had been told which would have been better left untold. The fact of Nelson's connection with Lady Hamilton had been known, the reviewers assumed, to many; but the documentation of the attachment was still a national crime, for it made public and official a fact which, while oral, could be discounted as rumor. The gravity of this insult to national pride is reflected by the violence of the *Edinburgh* reviewer's language.

> The man who should violate the last hallowed retreat of his war-worn frame, and display, for hire, the naked and festering limbs of the departed hero to the gaze of the brutal multitude, would be guilty, we think, of a less profanation. The outrage against decency, and the offence to all generous feeling, would not at least be aggravated in such a case, as we cannot help fearing they are here, by the strangest ingratitude, and the most incredible breach of confidence: for who but *the receiver* of these letters could have the means of giving them to the public?[7]

6. Oman, pp. vii, 666–67.

7. Review of *The Letters of Lord Nelson to Lady Hamilton* (1814), *Edinburgh Review*, 23, 398.

There were a number of lesser offenses committed by this "reprehensible" publication. Nelson's opinions of several living contemporaries (some of them nobility, up to and including the Prince of Wales) were made current: "a pretty indiscriminate abuse of every man, woman and child, whom he has occasion to mention, except Sir William and Lady Hamilton and one or two of their common friends, not amounting in the whole to quite six privileged persons, make up the bulk, if not the whole, of his letters."[8] The objection was not that the editor had suppressed nothing, for he had announced in his preface that "some parts (though not very numerous)" had been "suppressed,"[9] but that he had not suppressed every reference to contemporaries or, better still, the entire correspondence.

> What will our readers think when we tell them that in these letters, so complimentary to the *elegant* and *delicate* Emma, other females of the highest rank and the purest characters in society are designated by appellations so vulgar, so gross, so indecent, that we cannot stain our paper with them, and can only describe them as belonging to the dialect of the most depraved profligates of both sexes; and these horrible passages, neither honour of the dead, nor tenderness for the living, nor respect for public decorum, has induced the editor (who however can obliterate on occasion) to expunge![1]

The *Edinburgh* reviewer, inevitably, sets forth the correspondence's disregard for the exemplary principle, and thus underlines the limitations of the principle as an artistic philosophy of biography:

> Without stating it formally as a proposition, that all men may do wrong, because a great man did so, . . . it is to be feared that the knowledge of his faults sooths many a con-

8. *Edinburgh Review*, 23 (1814), 401.

9. "Suppressed, from the most honourable *feelings to individuals,* as they would certainly have given pain" (*Letters of Lord Nelson,* advertisement, *1* [v]–vi).

1. *Quarterly Review, 11* (1814), 74. The passages to which the reviewer alludes are probably those of Nelson's letter of 16 February 1801: "Lady A.

science, and is made the salve to heal over those wholesome wounds, through which remorse might otherwise open an avenue to virtue. The public opinion, too, may be affected imperceptibly. . . . The community may cease to despise, with such undivided contempt, as it now does, the vile and degraded wretch, who maltreats her whom he has taken for better and for worse, and vowed to protect for life. The conduct most befitting a coward, an effeminate and besotted tyrant, may no longer call forth the unanimous execration of Englishmen, when they vaguely hear it said, that 'Nelson did so.'[2]

The reviewer goes on to say that "the only remedy" within his reach is free expression of indignation. The implication is that a better remedy, now put out of mind by publication, would have been suppression or destruction of the entire correspondence. Better that the public image of Nelson the hero had been passed on to posterity intact, with nothing to detract from its power for good but some early insubordination which turned out to be brilliant naval tactics. The chief regret of the reviewers is that heroism could be destroyed by publication.

The fame of Lord Nelson is, as his life and services were, public property; and we absolutely deny the right to which any unworthy possessor of a few of his private notes may pretend, to invade . . . that public property, and lower the reputation of the hero and his country. Lord Nelson's private letters to Lady Hamilton contain absolutely nothing to justify their publication. Of his public transactions, or of his private sentiments of public affairs they furnish no memorial;—they are the mere records of the transient clouds of his temper, of the passing feelings of his heart, of the peevishness, which an anxious spirit and a sickly frame produced: and if we are

___

is as damned a w—— as ever lived, and Mrs. W—— is a bawd! Mrs. U—— a foolish pimp; eat up with pride, that a P—— will condescend to put her to expence" (*Letters of Lord Nelson, 1,* 29).

2. *Edinburgh Review, 23* (1814), 404.

obliged, in truth and candour, though most reluctantly, to say that they are coarse, shallow, and fulsome, miserably deficient in taste, ease, or amiability, let us not be accused of endeavouring . . . to degrade a name which we love almost to idolatry: our real motives are a true anxiety for his fame, and a desire to extinguish at once these base attempts at *turning a penny* by the prostitution of so noble a name, and the betraying of so high a confidence.[3]

Discretion, it was thought, would certainly have been the better part of valor.

Although the critics generally assert that the value to the public of exemplary lives of Nelson far outweighed whatever new insights these letters cast upon the man behind the hero, the *Edinburgh* reviewer does admit that the letters depict a new side of Nelson. The hero sat down "to throw upon his paper all that was in his heart,"[4] and "every here and there we see traits of some friendship almost as warm as the passion which has dictated the bulk of the correspondence."[5] But such revelations are "meagre of almost every thing like thinking":[6] they depict Nelson "idling his time away."[7] The *Quarterly* reviewer even admits that the letters present a characteristic Nelson, but he still would have preferred suppression.

We knew Lord Nelson, and we saw in him abundant reason to excuse, almost to forget these little imperfections of his noble nature—but even those who knew him not, or, we should rather say, even those who only know him by his great achievements and generous spirit will be prepared, from their own knowledge of human nature, to expect that so much zeal, such an ardent enthusiasm, such a self-devouring anxiety as prompted him in his career of glory, would not have been unaccompanied by a certain impatience of

3. *Quarterly Review, 11* (1814), 73.
4. *Edinburgh Review, 23* (1814), 401.
5. Ibid., p. 406.
6. Ibid., p. 402.
7. Ibid., p. 401.

feeling and a certain freedom of expression which were naturally pardonable, indeed almost admirable, in the man himself, but which it is grievous to every honest heart, and injurious to the human character to have recorded, chronicled, and exposed.[8]

The *Edinburgh* reviewer grudgingly recognized that, once published, the letters were "matter of history, and must pass as such into the records of the age,"[9] but he did not know that this "reprehensible publication" better served the cause of biography than most of the respectable exemplary publications. Thomas Pettigrew consulted the original letters, but after he had used some extracts from them for his life of Nelson, the manuscripts disappeared.[1] What we know of this side of Nelson's life depends to a great extent on this publication, undertaken to "turn a penny."

It is difficult for us to understand today what difference publication of the letters made to Nelson's reputation. The attachment to Lady Hamilton was known; Nelson's treatment of his wife was notorious. It is as if knowledge did not become fact until published in octavo. Many other considerations were involved, but it gives pause to reflect that Nelson (his improprieties not yet authenticated in print) was buried in St. Paul's, while Byron (whose improprieties had been widely circulated in printed form) was refused the Abbey.

In the destruction of Lord Byron's memoirs, most of the objections that the Nelson letters evoked in public were voiced in private. The circumstances surrounding the incident seem too familiar to require here a detailed narrative or an analysis of the complex personal motives behind the arguments of each of the participants.[2] A summary of the reasons put forward in

8. *Quarterly Review, 11* (1814), 73–74.

9. *Edinburgh Review, 23* (1814), 399.

1. Pettigrew's book was published in 1849 (*Memoirs of the Life of Vice-Admiral Lord Viscount Nelson*, 2 vols.). Oman comments on the loss of the MSS (pp. vii, 683).

2. The most complete account may be found in Leslie A. Marchand's *Byron* (1957), 3, 1245–53, and Doris Langley Moore's "The Burning of

the discussions which preceded this literary auto-da-fé should be enough to indicate their connection with the trends and principles discussed in this chapter.

John Cam Hobhouse led the campaign for destruction and made clear from the start (almost from the moment he heard of Byron's death) what motivated him: "After the first access of grief was over I then determined to lose no time in doing my duty by preserving all that was left to me of my friend—his fame— My thoughts were turned to the Memoirs of his life given to Thomas Moore."[3] His aims were the salvation of the fame and reputation Byron retained at his death, the maintenance of this public image without further self-incrimination of moral character, and the prevention of further discussion of the separation from Lady Byron and its causes. Destruction of the memoirs would guarantee that the memory of Byron in Greece would not be "lowered" by these earlier revelations.

Hobhouse was pleasantly surprised by Murray's wholehearted agreement, not just in the necessity of destruction, but also in the principle which justified destruction. "Such regard have I for Lord Byron's fame and honour that I am willing and am determined to destroy these MSS which have been read by Mr Gifford, who says that they would render Lord Byron's name eternally infamous."[4] Gifford's opinion was stated in somewhat stronger terms than Murray indicates. Hobhouse

---

Byron's Memoirs," in *The Atlantic Monthly, 204* (1959), 27–37, and *The Late Lord Byron* (1961), passim. G. Wilson Knight's highly interesting and imaginative reconstruction of the contents of the memoirs also contains detailed discussion of the events leading up to the destruction (*Lord Byron's Marriage*, 1957, passim), and his conclusions depend, to a great extent, upon his interpretation of the arguments set forth prior to the burning. The major contemporary sources for these narratives are cited in these works, so it seems hardly necessary to repeat them here.

3. Hobhouse's diary, quoted in Marchand, *3,* 1244.

4. Hobhouse's record of Murray's speech at the meeting in Hobhouse's Albany rooms, prior to the meeting at the bookseller's home where the destruction took place; quoted from Hobhouse's *Narrative* (Murray MSS) by Doris Langley Moore, *The Late Lord Byron* (1961), p. 33.

quoted him as saying "that the whole Memoirs was fit only for a brothel and would doom Lord B to everlasting infamy if published."[5]

Thomas Moore, sometime owner of the manuscript, proved the real stumbling-block to Hobhouse's plan for destruction. He felt that burning the memoirs without reading them[6] "would be throwing a stigma upon the work, which it did not deserve"[7]—a stigma which later materialized, as reviewers of Moore's life of Byron demonstrated by assuming the most evil possible contents. At this time, however, even Moore did not expect or desire the publication of the memoirs in toto but hoped to avoid destruction so that he could include portions of the account in his projected life of Byron. He agreed to consult Byron's sister: "the manuscript . . . should be placed in her hands, to be disposed of as she should think proper."[8] Some commentators have perhaps exaggerated Lady Byron's influence in the destruction, but it is clear that consideration of the family's feelings—that is, the feelings of both Lady Byron and Mrs. Leigh—was second only to the preservation of Byron's fame in the minds of the members of this strange committee. At one point during the crucial meeting, Moore proposed a compromise to Wilmot Horton (Lady Byron's representative) which would have taken full account of family sensitivity: "that every object might be gained by our perusing and examining it together . . . and, rejecting all that could wound the feelings of a single individual, but preserving what was innoxious and creditable to Lord Byron, of which I assured him there was a considerable proportion."[9] The family, however (as was inevitable from the start), found destruction the

5. Hobhouse's diary, 15 May 1824, quoted in Marchand, *3*, 1246.

6. They had been widely read, according to G. Wilson Knight (*Lord Byron's Marriage*, 1957, pp. 150–55). Moore was afraid that the original might be worn out as it passed from one set of "honourable hands" to the next (ibid., p. 151).

7. Thomas Moore, *Memoirs, Journal, and Correspondence*, ed. Lord John Russell (8 vols. 1853–56), *4*, 188.

8. Ibid., *4*, 189.

9. Ibid., *4*, 190–91.

only safe course. Mrs. Leigh was somewhat pained at "the horrid task assigned" her—to make the decision for burning—but concurred in principle: "much as I agree in the expediency of the destruction of this or any thing that may be a disgrace to poor B[']s memory."[1]

"Poor B" himself seems never to have overestimated the public's moral threshold for his revelations. He recognized that the work was "too sincere" in spots, but hoped that "tastes may change."[2] There is some indication by Thomas Moore, both before and after the destruction, that Byron had had even more misgivings about eventual publication. In the words of the second deed for the sale of the memoirs, drawn up between Moore and Murray, 6 May 1822, "Lord Byron and Mr. Moore are now inclined to wish the said work not to be published."[3] After the burning, Moore used this hint (or Byron's second thoughts, if he did in truth express any) to excuse his part in the destruction of the manuscript. He records that Hobhouse had reminded him that Byron had ultimately regretted giving away his memoirs. "This," wrote Moore, "if I wanted any justification to myself for what I have done, would abundantly satisfy me as to the propriety of the sacrifice."[4]

The literary periodicals recorded slight discomfort upon hearing that a literary work of a major figure of the age had been destroyed, but were immediately comforted when they were "informed that the omitted fragments consisted chiefly of satirical portraits of living persons, and it must, therefore, be at once admitted that in consigning them to the flames, Mr. Moore exercised a sound as well as an honourable discretion."[5]

1. Letter to Lady Byron dated "Sunday night," from Lovelace Papers, quoted in Doris Langley Moore, p. 25.
2. Byron's *Letters and Journals*, ed. R. E. Prothero (1898–1901 and later), 5, 131, 212.
3. Quoted by Marchand from a quotation of the deed in Murray's letter to Wilmot Horton, 19 May 1824 (Marchand, *3*, 1245 n.).
4. Moore's diary, quoted in Doris Langley Moore, p. 36.
5. Review of Moore's *Letters and Journals of Lord Byron*, Vol. 1 (1830), *Monthly Review*, III, *13*, 218.

It is impossible to understand this incident fully without the knowledge of just what revelations were suppressed. Perhaps, as G. Wilson Knight asserts, the memoirs contained a clear statement of Byron's "marriage secret," or of his latent or overt homosexuality. On the other hand, the memoirs need not have been that revealing or sensational to have provoked violent disturbance among Byron's friends and relatives. A simple narrative of his early life would have been sufficient, or, for that matter, a clearly autobiographical statement of some of the thinly fictionalized incidents of his poems.[6] Dignity and example imposed a severe rule upon any kind of personal revelation.

The exemplary principle and the doctrine of dignity combined to produce an atmosphere favorable to suppression and the logical rationale for its practice. Yet another element, involved in both the atmosphere and the rationale, was the force which reviewers designate "public propriety." It seems to have been a product of other forces rather than a force in itself, but it was necessary for some of the arguments of the doctrine of dignity and all those of the exemplary principle. "Public propriety" perhaps never existed anywhere but in the minds of a few critics, but it was manifested there as a universal sensitivity to strong words, violent or vicious actions, and wicked lives. It was the writer's consciousness of the tender minds of young ladies who might peruse his book, and the critic's awareness of how far the limits of decency could be stretched. This spectre, an intangible presence which emulated virtue and recoiled in revulsion from the verbal depiction of any sort of vice, had not yet attained its full potential, but many men of influence in the world of letters believed in it with a conviction accorded only to moral principle. It sat at Thomas Bowdler's elbow as he produced the *Family Shakespeare*. It dictated a few of John ("the most timid of God's booksellers") Murray's letters to

6. For a conservative and well-documented estimate of the nature of the memoirs, see Doris Langley Moore, pp. 46–53.

Byron. In it can be found a key to the recurring use of "utility" so prevalent in criticism, and some explanation for the continual attack on "low curiosity" and "vulgar scandal." With the aid of attendant spirits of exemplary biography and the doctrine of dignity, it scattered asterisks through biography as God had scattered stars in the heavens.

To a certain extent, the development of the concept at this time was, as I have already suggested, influenced by the number of new readers. References to "the average reader" and "the mass of mankind" turn up in reviews again and again. It was felt that unsophisticated minds ought not to be left on their own; they could not distinguish vice unless it was stigmatized, or virtue unless it was adequately applauded. Literature and biography were no longer for the sagacious and sophisticated few; they had to be reformed for the inexperienced and naïve many.

John Wilson Croker, writing in the *Quarterly,* gave a clear indication of the course which the combination of exemplary biography, the doctrine of dignity, extreme contemporaneity, and the consideration of public propriety was imposing upon the art of biography, and the dangers it presented to the standards of historical truth.

Whether a man writes his own life or that of some dear friend lately deceased, it is evident that there must be such a favourable colour spread over the picture that its fidelity must be rather worse than dubious. . . . Unfavourable or discreditable circumstances are generally passed over in silence, or if they should be of too much notoriety to be wholly unnoticed, they are so covered by the veil of partiality as hardly to be recognized. We have on our table Memoirs of Robespierre, . . . in which the leading feature of his character is said to have been the most sensitive humanity and an almost morbid aversion to the shedding of blood. To crimes—at least to such as those of Robespierre—there is no great danger that the indignation of the reader should be mitigated by the partiality of a biographer; but there are many minor frailties of a man's character which ought *in justice* to be told, but which one would be unwilling to drag back to public notice while his better qualities are still fresh and fragrant in the memory and affection of his family and acquaintance. But the grave has scarcely been closed over such a man, when the amiable partiality, or the calculating prudence, of his friends puts forth a Life, in which these questionable topics are either altogether omitted or kindly misrepresented. If any one—roused by what he thinks undeserved praise—should be so fearless a lover of truth as to endeavour to set the matter in its true point of view, he would have against him not merely the clamours and complaints of the surviving family, but even the good-natured sympathy of the public—who would say, *'It is all very true—but it was long ago, 'tis now forgotten—why revive it?—and, after all, the rest of his life was so respectable and amiable!'* On the other hand, if no notice be taken of such circumstances, the uncontradicted panegyric will be hereafter taken for *undeniable* truth; and other persons, whose conduct towards the individual might have been guided by a knowledge of such circumstances, will pass down to posterity with the reproach of having been negligent, or ungrateful, or envious—when, if the truth were known, they would appear perhaps to have acted with indulgence, delicacy, and honour.[7]

Croker's prophecies bore full fruit later in the century: objectivity declined as the "official" biographer came to the fore. It was the natural result of the substitution of dignified omission for artistic selectivity, and the triumph of "proper" suppression over truth.

The doctrines and the rules applied not only to the bad or average lives: each of the three most significant biographers— Southey, Moore, and Lockhart—made his separate peace with contemporary principles. All three contain suppression, all manifest some respect for dignified distance, all are conscious

7. Review of *Memoirs of the Life of . . . Sir James Mackintosh* (1835), *Quarterly Review, 54,* 251–52.

of example. The best in biography did not ignore contemporary dogmas, but found a way to live with them.

In our smug post-Freudian view of nineteenth-century timidity, the example of Stevenson and the similar (and more recent) example in lives of Norman Douglas should remind us that biography is not yet completely free of suppression. We do not care to remember that some suppression, or at least discreet selectivity, is always necessary for the contemporaneous biographer. Were the public furor of the *Letters to Lord Nelson* brought up to date—were they letters to Winston Churchill—theft would still be necessary for publication, and *The Spectator* and the *Saturday Review* would protest such publication in terms not unlike those which the *Critical* and *Quarterly* applied to the Nelson letters.

Nevertheless, nineteenth-century suppression was more extreme than ours. For the most part, we have returned to the biographer the responsibility for discretion. The feelings of the living, the fame and reputation of the dead still have a potent force, but we do not feel it necessary to compile general doctrinal rules governing the use of personal documents. Asterisks are no longer scattered with such abandon, but fame and reputation of the recently dead seem to get their due in reasonable, if silent, respect.

HIGHER CRITICISM:
STANFIELD AND CARLYLE

Survey historians tend to characterize nineteenth-century biography by contrapuntal quotation of Macaulay and Carlyle. In one sense, this is wise: to compound a critical theory from snippets of the periodical reviewers would produce only nonsense. They never passed up an opportunity to expand particular failings of a book into a sweeping characterization or denunciation of the whole literature (or, occasionally, of the whole United Kingdom), but they seldom saw the books before them clearly enough to conceive of an art of biography. If a contemporary theory of biography existed, it must be found in higher criticism—that which envisioned criteria for a kind of biography which did not exist but was feasible, that which went beyond strictures on extant biography to point out productive avenues for future biographers. Macaulay, Carlyle, and James Field Stanfield all attempted such criticism.

Macaulay can be eliminated rather quickly. His strictures on Boswell's *Johnson* are antiliterary (there *is* no art of biography), and are pursued along the worst ad hominem lines of contemporary reviewing.[1] He is the leading spokesman of the

---

1. "Many persons who have conducted themselves foolishly in active life, and whose conversation has indicated no superior powers of mind, have

notion that the only art of biography is to be found in the subject's sense of the art of life. In asserting that Boswell's folly produced a great book, Macaulay destroys the usefulness of his principles. If there is no creator, there can be no literary art.

James Field Stanfield comes to biography and to criticism little equipped to speak with authority on either. He was educated for the Roman Catholic priesthood, involved in the slave traffic at sea, and later became an abolitionist, director of a small theatrical company, and writer of comic opera, a propagandized travel book, a didactic poem, but never a biography.[2] He had no literary connections[3] and wrote no reviews, but in the midst of this frenetic career he seems to have found time to read widely in biography and biographical literature and to have undertaken as a true amateur a study of science and scientific method. His *Essay on the Study and Composition of Biography*[4] is an attempt to unite both of his amateur enthusiasms into a new science. Biography, he felt, was a study of man in individual manifestations. Systematized, might it not become a humanistic science, infinitely more important than biology?

Far from hitting this idealistic mark, Stanfield's *Essay* has

---

written valuable works. . . . But these men attained literary eminence in spite of their weaknesses. Boswell attained it by reason of his weakness. If he had not been a great fool, he would never have been a great writer. . . . Of the talents which ordinarily raise men to eminence as writers, he had absolutely none. . . . He had, indeed, a quick observation and a retentive memory. These qualities, if he had been a man of sense and virtue, would scarcely of themselves have sufficed to make him conspicuous; but, as he was a dunce, a parasite, and a coxcomb, they have made him immortal" (review of Croker's edition of Boswell's *Life of Johnson*, in *Edinburgh Review, 54*, 1831, 17–18).

2. *Dictionary of National Biography* (1898), 53, 476–78.

3. His son, Clarkson Stanfield, had privileges his father did not: as a recognized painter of marine landscapes he was called in by Charles Dickens to paint drops for his amateur theatricals.

4. Published by a provincial house (Gale, Curtis and Fenner) in Sunderland. Library of Congress and British Museum have copies.

been almost completely forgotten.[5] His system and scientific method deserve the neglect. A necessary premise of his theory is that, as a scientific art, biography is perfectible; that by derivation of select rules from the methods of skillful biographers of the past, by distillation of their variety and complexity into highly limited and clearly defined method, it is possible (with patience and adherence to the system) not just to create a perfect biography, but to arrive at the scientific method for all biography. Stanfield's belief in perfectibility is just as firm and as hopelessly optimistic as Matthew Arnold's conviction that there would eventually be a perfect translation of Homer.

Had Boswell adopted Stanfield's system, he would not have produced (as Stanfield implies) a more coherent life of Johnson (tempering the "egotism, culpable concealments, and indiscriminate admiration"[6] of the original) but rather a shorter, duller, conventional book. But Stanfield's *Essay* cannot be dismissed out of hand on the merits of probable products of its method. In the process of outlining a ridiculously involved system in a prose style not only tedious but confusing, Stanfield consistently introduces vital questions of biographical art. He attempts to find a balance between scientific objectivity and high moral example, between the historian's dignified distance and the biologist's microscopic interest in all available data, between the external appearance of public image and the internal springs of intimate personality.

Carlyle's theory has inspirational peaks and memorable figures; Stanfield's offers, at best, only a realistic concern with the practical problems of biography. He proposes a solution for every problem, and if his solutions fail, his recognition and description of the problems are remarkable. His theory is firmly rooted in his age, and as he is more practical than Carlyle, so is he at times a better reflection of theory in that age.

5. Francis R. Hart recognized the importance of Stanfield's *Essay* and quotes extensively from it in his article "Boswell and the Romantics," *ELH*, 27 (1960), 44.

6. *Essay* (1813), p. 63. Subsequent references are cited within parentheses in the text.

Proximity is the keystone of Stanfield's theory.

> The assumption of character must be complete. Our own
> state and peculiar opinions must, for the moment, be aban-
> doned, and the condition of the character, we wish to conceive
> or represent, wholly engage us;—totus in hoc. Such a force
> of imagination is to be acquired, that we are to see, not with
> our own, but with our hero's eyes, and feel only with his
> faculties; we must contract his habits, adopt his manners, as-
> sume his sentiments, invest ourselves with his partialities and
> humours; be actuated by his motives, guided by his designs,
> and elated by his attainments (122).

Having invested himself with the character of his subject (very
much in the manner of the method actor), the biographer proceeds to a course of general and particular reading, to the
drawing up of tables,[7] to the definition of a ruling passion.
Once he has collected this data and prepared himself, though,
he must deal with matters which cannot be reduced to tables.

The most important of these is the "biographical spirit,"
"that peculiar taste, that inclination, that earnestness, . . . that
obvious and continued warmth, which excites our sympathy,
and that conscious elevation of intelligence, which gives confidence to our application" (21). The spirit is pervasive: it
extends beyond the biographer's own enthusiasm for the subject and becomes a connective force which unites the distant
poles and opposing principles which make biography so difficult. The "biographical spirit" is a state of mind in the biographer which he transfers to his work, giving it life, ultimately
conveyed to his reader. Thus the reader receives a direct enthusiasm for the subject, for man's life as a whole.

> Like the spirit of animation, its effects are various. Among
> other manifestations, . . . there is brought before us a lively

7. The "Table of the First Order" describes the characteristic manners,
actions, motives, advantages, and disadvantages of six ages of man. The
subject is scored in each age against other men at corresponding times. The
"Table of the Second Order" is a series of maxims, mottoes, and bromides
(e.g. "Without the supply of talent, ambition is impotent; without opportunity, useless," p. 94). The precise use of these is obscure.

description of appearances, indicating, at the same time, . . . the laws by which these appearances are shaped and governed; sometimes in an interesting, continued series of action; sometimes in delicate circumstances of situation and sentiment; but, most of all, in those eventful occurrences, where the soul appears through the action, and character is developed at a single stroke;—not exactly the sublime of rhetoricians, but always resembling it, in exciting an emotion in the reader, proportionate to that which animates the sensibility and expression of the author (108).

By citing the necessity of enthusiasm to the "biographical spirit," Stanfield grudgingly admits that there is a nonscientific element involved. He insists, however, that the "spirit" is not a gift of the Muse but a philosophic understanding of human nature.

This biographical spirit is not . . . a matter that comes at once upon the mind like a gift of inspiration. It can be only acquired by patient study and habitual reflection, and by the facility and affection generated in the process. The principles, the divisions, and the relative connections of general biography . . . must be ever present, and continually brought to bear upon the subjects of observation; until, by a perseverance in the practice, they will insensibly unite with the other mental acquisitions and faculties; and, when forgotten in their terms, like the rules of grammar and logic, will, silently, modify and direct the acuteness of our conceptions and researches (111–12).

The study of human nature acts in a manner similar to Wordsworth's powers of nature: the matter of the study may be forgotten, but its effect remains.[8] Stanfield perhaps confuses the issue of biographical art with scientific considerations, but he offers an explanation for the faculty that is essentially artistic.

8. The latter section of the passage quoted above shows, almost unmistakably, the influence of David Hartley. Hartley's theories also appear in Stanfield's description of the ages of man (pp. 202–74).

The "biographical spirit" connects dissimilar motives and events, selects telling details, and creates a balance between objective, scientific truth and ethical example (a balance biographers of the early nineteenth century could never achieve in practice). Stanfield does not attempt to draw up a table or a set of practical steps leading to such a balance, but simply asserts that the "delightful" powers of the "biographical spirit" must never lose sight of the "valuable" and "important" duties of the biographer.[9] To philosophy, which has given him the "biographical spirit," and to literary skill, which has given him the power to select relevant and telling details, must be added "sound ethical knowledge and principles, with a mind qualified to discern the existence, and a heart fitted to approve the worth of moral action" (83). His scientific principles will not admit suppression for ethical reasons as a possibility, but the biographer still has a duty to "judge" his subject.

Despite Stanfield's scientific apparatus, despite his impossible balances and his blind faith in systematic perfectibility, his major concern in the *Essay* was artistic. Biography, he felt, was being swallowed by side issues and nonartistic doctrines. He deplored the failings of the automatic biographer: slavish adherence to chronology, the profusion of irrelevant and pointless anecdotes, the general decline in the biographer's responsibility (190–91, 60, xvi). He proclaimed, in his own wooden way, the importance of the biographer's composing hand. Were Stanfield's requirements for the biographer applied to Southey or Lockhart, their scientific or ethical failings would not be revealed, but rather the distance by which the biographer's art surpasses definition, legislation, or scientific method. But Stanfield did see contemporary dilemmas of biography and saw them whole, something few others even attempted.

The danger of confusing Thomas Carlyle's early biographical criticism with Macaulay's negativism lies in a few similarities in their strictures upon Croker's edition of Boswell. Carlyle's

---

9. This balance is discussed in *Essay*, pp. 332–33.

conviction that a man's life, properly written, is the logical extension and (in some cases, like Johnson's) the masterwork of his writings seems not far removed from Macaulay's corollary, that Boswell "would infallibly have made his hero as contemptible as he has made himself, had not his hero really possessed some moral and intellectual qualities of a very high order."[1]

Carlyle's and Macaulay's principles were forged of the same stuff. On one point, the necessity that a great biography have a great subject, they agree.[2] But there the similarity ends. Macaulay denies the biographer's art; Carlyle insists upon it as the only medium for the revelation of the subject's greatest work. Carlyle believes in the biographer's creativity, and forms his principles upon this belief. Macaulay believes in the pervasive power of the art of life and its ability to shine through narration by a fool.

The crux of this basic theoretical difference is revealed in their treatments of Boswell's personality. Macaulay's version is well known, and Boswell's reputation suffered under its onus for almost a century. Carlyle's judgment is perhaps improperly understood. Seen in isolation, his high respect for Boswell's "open, loving heart" seems to damn with faint praise, or, at best, to be merely "appreciative" in the worst sense. In the context of the whole plan and intent of his early biographical criticism, however, it is everything.

A concept which determined the course of many of his later writings and his own biographies is at the core of Carlyle's theory:[3] biography must relate man to society; courage is the fundamental measure of human character, and the subject can be measured only by how he uses it to face the world and his

---

1. Macaulay, review of Boswell, *Edinburgh Review, 54* (1831), 20.

2. Ibid. Carlyle implies this in review of Lockhart's *Burns*, quoted below, p. 73.

3. By 1838, the terminal date of this study, Carlyle had produced only his *Life of Schiller* (1825), and *The French Revolution* (1837) which was not strictly biographical.

fellow man. The theme is announced in 1827, in his review of Lockhart's *Burns*.

The problem of Burns's Biography has [not] yet been adequately solved. We do not allude so much to deficiency of facts or documents . . . as to the limited and imperfect application of them to the great end of Biography. Our notions upon this subject may perhaps appear extravagant; but if an individual is really of consequence enough to have his life and character recorded for public remembrance, we have always been of opinion, that the public ought to be made acquainted with all the inward springs and relations of his character. How did the world and man's life, from his particular position, represent themselves to his mind? How did co-existing circumstances modify him from without; how did he modify these from within? With what endeavours and what efficacy rule over them; with what resistance and what suffering sink under them? In one word, what and how produced was the effect of society on him; what and how produced was his effect on society? He who should answer these questions, in regard to any individual, would, as we believe, furnish a model of perfection in biography.[4]

The inherent conflict resembles one of Stanfield's requirements, the balance between the internal and external character, but Carlyle's "battle" is more involved with society and history. It not only provides the dynamism of conflict which Carlyle

4. Review of John Gibson Lockhart's *Life of Burns* (1828), *Edinburgh Review*, *48*, 269–70. In other essays, "society," "the world," and "environment" are used almost interchangeably. The concept was not just a device but was at the heart of Carlyle's social criticism: "To understand man, however, we must look beyond the individual man and his actions or interests, and view him in combination with his fellows. It is in Society that man first feels what he is; first becomes what he can be. In Society an altogether new set of spiritual activities are evolved in him, and the old immeasurably quickened and strengthened" ("Characteristics," a review of Hope's *An Essay on the Origin and Prospects of Man*, 1831, and Von Schlegel's *Philosophische Vorlesungen*, 1830, in *Edinburgh Review*, *54*, 359).

finds necessary in art, but also establishes a workable relationship between biography and narrative history.

In response to Carlyle's rhetorical question, "Of history, . . . is not the whole purport biographic?" man's battle with his surroundings offers a ready answer.

> What hope have we, except the for most part fallacious one of gaining some acquaintance with our fellow-creatures, though dead and vanished, yet dear to us; how they got along in those old days, suffering and doing; to what extent, and under what circumstances, they resisted the Devil and triumphed over him, or struck their colors to him, and were trodden under foot by him; how, in short, the perennial Battle went, which men name Life, which we also in these new days, with indifferent fortune, have to fight, and must bequeath to our sons and grandsons to go on fighting,— till . . . the Volume of Universal History wind itself up![5]

This all-inclusive view of history carried with it an implied moral view, based in a fundamental respect for the indomitable will: man's triumph in the "battle" was his virtue, his defeat was his evil.

> The Dead are all holy, even they that were base and wicked while alive. Their baseness and wickedness was not *They,* was but the heavy unmanageable Environment that lay round them, with which they fought unprevailing: *they* (the ethereal God-given Force that dwelt in them, and was their *Self*) have now shuffled off that heavy Environment, and are free and pure: their life-long Battle, go how it might, is all ended, with many wounds or with fewer; they have been recalled from it.[6]

Carlyle also saw a moral value—something almost sacred— in the biographer's re-creation of the "battle." It accomplished for the hero what he was not able to do for himself. The biographer was a chronicler: his subject's place in history and

5. "Biography," *Fraser's Magazine,* 5 (1832), 254.
6. Ibid., p. 258.

the revelation of a significant portion of his life's work depended upon the biographer's narration. Not only did the biographer have to judge accurately the power of environment and the force of the subject's will, but he had to write about them in such a way that a balance was achieved between internal will and external force.

In Currie's and Walker's biographies of Burns,[7] Carlyle saw failure resulting from an underestimation of the role of biography. Far from establishing a balance for the battle, neither even knew that such a battle had taken place.

> Dr Currie and Mr Walker . . . have both . . . mistaken one essentially important thing: Their own and the world's true relation to their author, and the style in which it became such men to think and to speak of such a man. . . . Both err alike in presenting us with a detached catalogue of his several supposed attributes, virtues, and vices, instead of a delineation of the resulting character as a living unity. This . . . is not painting a portrait; but gauging the length and breadth of the several features, and jotting down their dimensions in arithmetical ciphers. Nay, it is not so much as this: for we are yet to learn by what arts or instruments the mind *could* be so measured and gauged.[8]

Accurate judgment was useless without the essential balance.

Carlyle praises Lockhart's *Life of Burns* for its "sense of the whole": Lockhart "avoided the method of separate generalities, and rather sought for characteristic incidents, habits, actions, sayings; in a word, for aspects which exhibit the whole man, as he looked and lived among his fellows."[9] This position corresponds closely to Stanfield's insistence that the biographer keep the subject's general character before him at all times.[1]

7. James Currie, life prefixed to *Works* (1800); see Stauffer, p. 65. Josiah Walker, memoir prefaced to Burns' *Poems* (1811).

8. Review of Lockhart's *Life of Burns* (1828), in *Edinburgh Review, 48,* 268–69.

9. Ibid., p. 269.

1. "The position we would wish to establish is, that the character should not for a moment be lost to the artist's . . . view" (*Essay*, 1813, pp. 275–76).

Carlyle arrives almost intuitively at the method by which the biographer may achieve a balance of internal and external forces. True depiction of both depended upon clarity and concreteness of narrative. Carlyle believed in the perfectibility of biography.

It is well worth the Artist's while to examine for himself what it is that gives such pitiful incidents their memorableness; his aim likewise is, above all things, to be *memorable.* Half the effect . . . depends on the object; on its being *real,* on its being really *seen.* The other half will depend on the observer; and the question now is: How are real objects to be *so* seen; on what quality of observing, or of style in describing, does this so intense pictorial power depend? Often a slight circumstance contributes curiously to the result: some little, and perhaps to appearance accidental, feature is presented; a light-gleam, which instantaneously *excites* the mind, and urges it to complete the picture, and evolve the meaning thereof for itself. . . . The power to produce such [light-gleams], to select such features as will produce them, is generally treated as a knack, or trick of the trade, a secret for being "graphic;" whereas these magical feats are, in truth, rather inspirations; and the gift of performing them, which acts unconsciously, without forethought, and as if by nature alone, is properly a *genius* for description.[2]

After such a buildup, we are ready for Carlyle to reveal to the world once for all the secret of Boswell's art and the secret art of all factual narrative. But what follows demonstrates, perhaps more clearly than any other passage in Carlyle's essays, why he so often disappoints us: his insight fails to satisfy the expectation produced by the momentum of his words. His synthesis is an inspirational oversimplification which comes dangerously close to undermining his whole theory of biography.

One grand, invaluable secret there is, however, which includes all the rest, and, what is comfortable, lies clearly in

2. "Biography," pp. 258–59.

every man's power: *To have an open loving heart, and what follows from the possession of such!* ... This it is that opens the whole mind, quickens every faculty of the intellect to do its fit work, that of *knowing;* and therefrom, by sure consequence, of *vividly uttering forth.* Other secret for being "graphic" is there none, worth having: but this is an all-sufficient one.[3]

If at this point Carlyle forgets the whole for one of its parts in his eagerness to make all men eligible for biographical genius, in a more temperate moment he manages to set the "open, loving heart" in perspective. It seems to be a generalization designed to unify several more particular skills or qualities of the biographer: "Boswell wrote a good Book because he had a heart and an eye to discern Wisdom, and an utterance to render it forth; because of his free insight, his lively talent, above all, of his Love and childlike Open-mindedness."[4] The "open, loving heart" seems to be the same quality Stanfield was struggling to define in his discussion of the "biographical spirit." Carlyle assumes it is genius. Stanfield suggests an artistic explanation but backs off and concludes that it can only be attained by continual study. They are both groping for the same quality of artistic design and personal conviction, but Carlyle retires to a critical bromide and Stanfield retreats once again to his assumption that the art of biography must be scientific.

Even the oversimplification of the "open, loving heart" has indirect value to biographical theory, for upon it Carlyle constructs (in the ruins of his theory, if you will) a powerful and meaningful figure which comes perhaps as close as any to a workable figure for the biographer's art.

How indelible, and magically bright, does many a little *Reality* dwell in our remembrance! There is no need that the personages on the scene be a King and Clown; ... need only that the scene lie in this old firm Earth of ours, where we

3. Ibid., p. 259.
4. "On Boswell's Johnson," *Fraser's Magazine,* 5 (1832), 386.

also have so surprisingly arrived; that the personages be *men,* and *seen* with the eyes of a man. Foolish enough, how some slight, perhaps mean and even ugly incident (if *real,* and well presented) will fix itself in a susceptive memory, and lie ennobled there; silvered over with the pale cast of thought, with the pathos which belongs only to the Dead. . . . Hereby, indeed, is the whole man made a living mirror, wherein the wonders of this ever-wonderful Universe are, in their true light . . . represented, and reflected back on us. . . .

That loose-flowing, careless-looking Work of his is as a picture painted by one of Nature's own Artists; the best possible resemblance of a Reality; like the very image thereof in a clear mirror. Which indeed it was: let but the mirror be *clear,* this is the great point; the picture must and will be genuine. How the babbling Bozzy, inspired only by love, and the recognition and vision which love can lend, epitomises nightly the words of Wisdom, the deeds and aspects of Wisdom, and so, by little and little, unconsciously works together for us a whole *Johnsoniad;* a more free, perfect, sunlit, and spirit-speaking likeness, than for many centuries had been drawn by man of man! . . . Boswell's grand intellectual talent was (as such ever is) an *unconscious* one, of far higher reach and significance than Logic; and shewed itself in the whole, not in parts.[5]

The necessary reflector of the biographer, the vital third element in the concept of the "battle," completes Carlyle's theoretical system. If the hero's deeds are to be portrayed faithfully, so that any man at any time after may read of them and know the hero, they must be reflected by a contemporary mirror of reality not only capable of receiving the whole image of his subject, but also able to transmit directly in words the vividness, characteristics, and force of presence of his subject. His mind, "silvered over with the pale cast of thought," becomes the selective reflector, capturing momentary glimpses of the "light-

5. "Biography," pp. 258, 259; "On Boswell's Johnson," p. 385.

gleams." The "whole man" must be the mirror, and the mirror must be clear, for the "light-gleams" to be real.

The ultimate significance of reality so depicted is measured by the compounded standards of history and biography. Since the history Carlyle envisions is for the most part biographic, it is to be expected that an important function of biography will be historical. Not only does the biography give us Johnson, the hero long dead, reflected through the reverent eyes of Boswell, long closed; but the book gives a clear view of the total reality of their times, irrevocably passed away.

> For *Boswell's Life of Johnson* has Time done, is Time still doing, what no ornament of Art or Artifice could have done for it. Rough Samuel and sleek wheedling James *were,* and *are not.* Their Life and whole personal Environment has melted into air. . . . The mysterious River of Existence rushes on: a new Billow thereof has arrived, and lashes wildly as ever round the old embankments; but the former Billow with *its* loud, mad eddyings, where is it?—Where! Now this Book of Boswell's, this is precisely a Revocation of the Edict of Destiny; so that Time shall not utterly, not so soon by several centuries, have dominion over us. A little row of Naphtha-lamps, with its line of Naphtha-light, burns clear and holy through the dead Night of the Past: they who were gone are still here; though hidden they are revealed, though dead they yet speak. There it shines, that little miraculously lamp-lit Pathway, shedding its feebler and feebler twilight into the boundless dark Oblivion, for all that our Johnson *touched* has become illuminated for us: on which miraculous little Pathway we can still travel, and see wonders.[6]

Carlyle underestimates Boswell's work and overestimates the literary genius of Everyman's "open, loving heart" when he implies that the *Life of Johnson* was "unconscious." This does not, however, undercut his appreciation of biographical art. He places the responsibility for the art squarely upon the biog-

6. "On Boswell's Johnson," p. 387.

rapher's shoulders. This, which seems a truism now, was a significant critical act.

Carlyle was not unrealistic enough to assume that every biographer could satisfy his requirements, nor was he so cynical as to deny the usefulness of any biography which failed to meet his standards. The distinction between true biography and the "life" was that the former was composed, the latter only compiled. "Few individuals, indeed, can deserve such a study; and many *lives* will be written, and, for the gratification of innocent curiosity, ought to be written, and read, and forgotten, which are not in this sense *biographies*."[7]

"Such works," he felt, "may be something without being all."[8] His criterion for "composition" seems to have been brevity: the distinction between the compiler and the true biographer was in the thickness of the book. Thus he is put off by the length of Lockhart's *Scott*, but finally concludes that since it is, after all, but a compilation, the profuse documents and incidents do no harm. "The truth is, the work, done in this manner too, was good to have: Scott's Biography, if uncomposed, lies printed and indestructible here, in the elementary state, and can at any time be composed, if necessary, by whosoever has call to that."[9] He consoles himself that eventually all publishers will come to their senses and pay "literary men by the quantity they do *not* write."[1]

Both Stanfield and Carlyle were concerned with the shortcomings of contemporary biography: too many biographies were being compiled, too few were being composed. Both felt that the solution to contemporary problems lay in the biographer's artistic responsibility, which had been ignored by ad hoc criticism and diluted by nonartistic doctrines and dogmas. Carlyle

7. *Edinburgh Review*, *48* (1828), 270.

8. "Jean Paul Friedrich Richter Again," *Foreign Review*, printed in *Critical and Miscellaneous Essays* (1838), 2, 178.

9. Review of Lockhart's *Scott* in *London and Westminster Review*, *28* (1838), 298.

1. Ibid., p. 297.

saw the practical solution (if any of Carlyle's thundering intuitions can truly be called practical) in the biographer's historical perceptivity. The biographer had to realize his duty to posterity, and estimate his subject not by virtues or learning or talent but as a man in society. Stanfield saw a practical solution in the development of a "scientific" method of comparison which would treat each period in the subject's life in the context of specified rules for that time of life, a method which would systematize the comparison of one man's ultimate accomplishment with another's.

Both theories have obvious faults. Carlyle's "battle" is not appropriate as a central core for all subjects—it causes real difficulties when applied to an "insider," achieving his personal goals within the framework of, and in cooperation with, society. Stanfield simply did not have the scientific know-how or the terms of description to evolve the method he dimly conceived, much less to put it into practice. We perhaps have the know-how in modern psychology and psychoanalytic theory, but the book conceived by Stanfield has yet to be written. Nevertheless, both Carlyle and Stanfield saw a new challenge to biography in the complexities of a modern society. Man was now, in part at least, a product of his society, for he was involved in his society and society was a part of him throughout life in a manner not perceived by the eighteenth century. His individual piety, public action, or talent alone was not sufficient to merit biography. His perseverance in overcoming disadvantages to become successful in his individual field of endeavor was not enough. The whole man had to be measured by his total courage in confronting all the obstacles which the world put in his path.

This concern with the human values of the subject was a call to return to what Stauffer cites as the eighteenth century's ideal of "absolute faithfulness in representing life"[2]—but with the new factor of society added. Obsession with the dynamic conflict of man and society has been regarded as Carlyle's narrow prejudice, reflecting his personal taste in biography. As

2. Stauffer, *1*, 536.

it seems also to have been a meaningful issue to Stanfield earlier, it is perhaps more than personal preference.

Concern for subjects' personal courage is not an outstanding characteristic of most early nineteenth-century lives. But both Southey's *Nelson* and Lockhart's *Scott* have this concern; indeed, it is the core of each book. Southey, through portrayal of selected quirks and irregularities of Nelson, drew up the lines of the "battle" in terms of the human side of heroism; Lockhart, dealing with a basically unheroic subject, saw his problem to be the portrayal of the heroic side of Scott's human nature. Nelson was constantly opposed by society in the form of an "ungrateful nation." Scott's battle had more tragic overtones: as a combatant allied with the forces of society, he saw supposed comrades take up arms against him. A partisan of the conventional, he was struck down by the most conventional of society's weapons, financial loss. His battle was recovery from this blow.

The connection between theoretical criticism and practical composition is tenuous at best. There is probably no direct influence of critic upon biographer. If Lockhart had read Stanfield's book, he probably would have thought him a bad writer and a sorry critic. But the tenuous connection of mutual concern seems real enough. Stanfield with his academic graphs and tables, and Carlyle with his fiery inspirational sermons, called upon biographers to recognize and act upon artistic responsibility. Southey and Lockhart, each in his way, acted.

CHAPTER FIVE

SOUTHEY'S NELSON

O f more than fifty biographical productions[1] on Horatio Nelson's life, victories, and death published in the early nineteenth century, one is still widely read. Portions of it have been shown to be factually inaccurate,[2] its grasp of naval tactics has been declared woefully inadequate by a succession of naval historians,[3] a highly important correspondence not accessible at the time of writing has become available,[4] and many definitive studies of Nelson have been published, but this brief account is still read, reread, and republished.[5]

1. Based on *British Museum Catalogue*. Only 23 of these were lives; the rest were deathbed, battle, and funeral accounts, etc.

2. Cf. E. R. H. Harvey's edition of the *Life of Nelson* (1953), introduction and notes; and Carola Oman, *Nelson* (1947), bibliographical introduction, pp. [v]–x.

3. Harvey's edition (pp. xlv–lxi) discusses at length Geoffrey Callender's objections and suggestions for revision "in Nelson's interest." A. T. Mahan's *The Life of Nelson* (1897), although it does not attack Southey directly, does correct his narratives of the battles.

4. *The Letters of Lord Nelson to Lady Hamilton* (1814), discussed above, appeared the year after Southey's *Nelson* was first published.

5. William Haller in *The Early Life of Southey* (1917), p. 318, cites "no less than twenty-two" editions in England alone between 1843 and 1894. Jack Simmons, *Southey* (1948), p. 143, states that it was "reprinted at least a hundred times in England alone during the past century."

Popularity (even enduring popularity) can be evinced as an emblem of quality only with many qualifications. It is cited here as perhaps the most telling demonstration that the biographer's art cannot be judged in terms of the accuracy of its facts, its volume of materials, its definitive intent, or its exhaustive method. There is a creative art in tracing a life, in the plan and organization of its elements, in the creation of a living presence in words that is far more important.

Robert Southey did not set out with the high intent of constructing a biographical landmark: he was dragged to an unwilling effort. It came to him as a distraction from what he felt to be his serious literary work, his poetry. Four lives of Nelson[6] were forwarded to him from the *Quarterly* as part of his regular duty-packet of review books. He wrote a review which (in the manner of many contemporary reviews) contained his own brief biographical sketch of Nelson.

The review adhered to his accustomed line of biographical criticism. These books were too long and too heavy ("So ponderous a concern. . . . Is it to be supposed that they can possibly digest one-and-twenty pounds of biography, even when Nelson is the subject?");[7] or else they were undertaken with a misguided intent—to turn a penny ("hastily compiled for the sake of obtaining some temporary relief in his embarrasments") or to grind a particular axe ("friends . . . were in search of a writer who would undertake to justify the only culpable parts of his conduct").[8] Compilation was no substitute for composition ("They have professed to form a narrative, but the main part of the book consists of extracts . . ., so that it is rather a work of reference than a biographical composition").[9]

These points were not just ad hoc, spur-of-the-moment crit-

6. John Charnock, *Biographical Memoirs of* . . . *Nelson* (1806); James Harrison, *The Life of Lord Nelson* (1806); T. O. Churchill, *The Life of Lord Viscount Nelson* . . . (1808); and James Stanier Clarke and John M'Arthur, *The Life of Admiral Lord Nelson* . . . *from His Lordship's Manuscripts* (1809).

7. Southey's review, in *Quarterly Review, 3* (1810), 222.

8. Ibid., pp. 220, 221.

9. Ibid., p. 222.

icism. Brevity, simplicity, a connected and coherent narrative, and the necessity of a clear example had been articles of his biographical criticism in the *Annual Review*. Southey's systematic destruction of William Godwin's *Life of Chaucer* had denounced pointless voluminous compilation.

> Some centuries ago, when an author was about to write a book, he considered that all his readers were unlearned; that they who should read his volume had perhaps never read another; and, therefore, he usually gave them the whole stock of his knowledge, beginning generally with Adam, and so proceeding regularly down to his own subject. This is the case with Mr. Godwin: . . . taking it for granted that all who read his book were to be as ignorant as he was himself when he began to write it, he has therefore told them all he knows.[1]

Insistence upon the creativity of the biographer is a leading principle in most of Southey's reviews. The use of autobiographical materials might be the current fashion, but overdependence upon them could end in abdication of artistic responsibility.

> This [autobiographical] method is lively and entertaining, and carries with it a strong impression of authenticity; it has, however, obvious defects. . . . The thread of the narrative is broken, and all the proportion of length, to importance of matter, destroyed by such an intermixture. . . . We are persuaded, that it will seldom be employed, unless where the biographer is conscious of a paucity of materials for his own share of the work, or of some nice and delicate points in the story, upon which he does not choose to express himself with the responsibility of an author.[2]

With all of these principles, of course, Southey is exercising the prerogative of the critic to be critical. The test of his preach-

1. *Annual Review* (for 1803), 2, 464.
2. Review of William Hayley's *Life and Posthumous Writings of William Cowper, Annual Review* (for 1803), 2, 459.

ings is his own biographical method, but this proves to be surprisingly consistent with the principles from which he argued in criticism. The sketch in the *Quarterly* opened with an announcement of what he felt to be the ideal biographical approach to Nelson: "The best eulogium of Nelson is the history of his actions; the best history that which shall relate them most perspicuously."[3] After the review appeared, Murray contracted with him for its expansion into a small book, evidently convincing Southey that he should undertake further research and writing by an argument based on utility and the book's value for exemplary purposes. Southey described the projected work to Grosvenor Bradford as "such a life of Nelson as shall be put into the hands of every youth destined for the navy—a five-shilling volume, for which he gives me a hundred guineas."[4] By some publisher's mistake or change in plans, the book appeared in two volumes, which Southey felt would defeat its avowed purpose and "materially . . . injure the sale."[5] The first edition appeared in 1813, with a foreword proclaiming an unchanged exemplary intent.

> Many lives of Nelson have been written: one is yet wanting, clear and concise enough to become a manual for the young sailor, which he may carry about with him, till he has treasured up the example in his memory and in his heart. In attempting such a work, I shall write the eulogy of our great naval Hero: for the best eulogy of NELSON is the faithful history of his actions: and the best history, that which shall relate them most perspicuously.[6]

3. *Quarterly Review, 3* (1810), 224.
4. Bodleian MSS c. 24 fol. 134, quoted in Jack Simmons, *Southey* (1948), p. 142 and note; no date given. Southey eventually received £300 for *Nelson:* £100 each for the original *Quarterly* sketch, the book, and the republication in the Family Library (C. C. Southey's note, *Life and Correspondence,* 1849–50, *4, 17*).
5. Letter to John May, 3 Jan. 1813, ibid., *4, 6–7.*
6. *Life of Nelson* (1813), *1* [1]. Subsequent quotations from this work are given in parentheses.

The strength of Southey's *Nelson* is produced by both the best and worst biographical thought of its time, written partly in conformity to contemporary principles and partly in reaction against them. Southey's adherence to the exemplary principle sets his book in the central stream of biography usually characterized by conscience rather than art, piety rather than heroism. But he builds on Nelson's example in such a manner that it becomes an organizing and creative, rather than a normalizing and destructive, force. By emphasizing brevity, Southey registers his discontent with both the autobiographical fashion and the low ebb of the biographer's responsibility, the triumph of encyclopedic compilation over artistic composition. At the same time, however, his particular motive for brevity in this book is the maintenance of its utility as example, the preservation of its character as "a manual for the young sailor."

That his understanding of "example" differed from that of his contemporaries becomes apparent in reading the first few pages of his *Nelson*. In the opening chapter, young Horatio is shown on a bear hunt ignoring his commanding officer's orders (*I*, 15–17). As anecdote succeeds anecdote, it becomes clear that this story is included not just to demonstrate youthful exuberance but is the germ of a major characteristic of Nelson's nature —one which is to dominate the book. The bloodless child of the pietistic exemplary life may be guilty of one such insubordinate act, but he quickly reforms after this token expression and leads out his life in wholly proper, wholly virtuous monotony. Southey's Nelson—the essence of the man that he managed to extract from the twenty-one pounds of anecdote and document—never reforms, but is a direct extension of that boy. The example presented is, superficially considered, courage and heroism without reward; patriotism and hatred of the French. Considered more critically, it is the example of stubborn, rather self-centered individualism—the example of a man commanded by no one but himself, serving the cause of his nation's honor, but serving it (like Hotspur) more as honor than as nation.

Some contemporary critics saw that this was essentially a dangerous book, and criticized it accordingly. One of the highly offended critics of Lady Hamilton's correspondence with Nelson took time out from his righteous indignation to get in a lateral jab at Southey.

The impatience of command which we have noticed, leads to a remark respecting this great man's public life, not unworthy of notice. He seems to have been formed by nature not only for the highest station—but for no other; and to have been alike incapable of occasionally falling into a subordinate part, and of contenting himself with a share of any joint operation. Mr Southey, in his life of him, is perpetually throwing out insinuations against the other officers who refused to concur in all Nelson's projects; as if those distinguished characters were bound to disobey orders from home, in order to gratify the curiosity of this commodore— whose projects on shore would almost always have led to a mere experiment upon the bravery of English soldiers and sailors. . . . If every commanding officer had acted so completely for himself, and with such disregard of orders or combined plans from home; nay, if only a very few officers had acted so, the speedy ruin of our affairs must have ensued; the army and navy would have become one scene of confusion.[7]

The critic misinterpreted. He thought that Southey's vision of Nelson was a function of the biographer's singleminded dedication to his hero's glory and fame, the product of abject hero worship. It was not. Southey was following his own persuasion about Nelson. He sincerely felt that the best example to be made of Nelson was the clearest narrative of his actions. This insubordinate, irregular, human genius behind the hero was the "figure in the carpet" to Southey, and it was this essence that he was determined to extract from Clarke and M'Arthur's mountain.

Southey's practical biographical theory does not spring fullarmed from his critical principles, but rather develops the hints

7. Review of *The Letters of Lord Nelson to Lady Hamilton* (1814), *Edinburgh Review*, 23, 405.

provided by them. The autobiographical mode has been carried far enough. So too has the indiscreet violation of the subject's epistolary correspondence. The doctrine of dignity is a counterforce, but here again Southey does not accept the contemporary principle per se. He adapts it to his uses, and turns a basically ethical principle to his artistic ends. Since he is under no requirement of compendious compilation, he is free to excerpt whatever letters he chooses, and to use only passages which support his concept of Nelson's state of mind at a given moment. There is no necessity to print any letter in full.[8]

Southey's use of Nelson's letters is perhaps the most telling artistry of the book. Without "violating" the privacy of the addressees of the letters, he extracts sentences, paragraphs, phrases which reflect directly Nelson's frustration, bitterness, conviction, or determination, and often his ironic humor. He inserts them in his narrative with the skill of a dramatist. Detailing diplomatic or naval actions with the narrative sweep of the historian, Southey pauses to punctuate the general narrative with Nelson's personal reactions. In this broad context, individual bitterness or frustration, joy or conviction, has an impact which in itself establishes the book's remarkable balance between historical action and individual reaction, between public recognition (or indifference) and private frustration. It matters little to the reader that he is often not even informed of the identity of the correspondent, for Southey's constant image of Nelson's character dictates his selection, and all the extracts come from the same Nelson—Southey's Nelson. Southey's artistic vision gives the extracts a unity the letters in toto lack —a sense of the living presence that keeps Nelson's personality in the foreground of an eventful public life. In conjunction with the narration of events, they become the hero's personal annotation of his life. Southey takes only what he wants: the "Nelson touch" of personality, the speech of his mind.

Dignity is, of course, a two-edged sword. It would be critically

8. The single exception is Nelson's codicil to his will concerning the welfare of Lady Hamilton and Horatia, written just before Trafalgar (2, 243–45).

dishonest to praise Southey's success in an adaptation of dignity without mentioning another application of the doctrine which clearly resulted in serious suppression: his treatment of the business of Lady Hamilton.

In Nelson's first serious encounter with Emma, Southey treads a line hung rather precariously between admission of the real nature of the relationship and an obligation to call it friendship.

> Sir William and Lady Hamilton led the way. . . . They had seen Nelson only for a few days four years ago, but they then perceived in him that heroic spirit which was now so fully and gloriously manifested to the world. Emma Lady Hamilton, who from this time so greatly influenced his future life, was a woman whose personal accomplishments have seldom been equalled, and whose powers of mind were not less fascinating than her person. . . . By her influence the British fleet had obtained those supplies at Syracuse, without which, Nelson always asserted, the battle of Aboukir could not have been fought. During the long interval which passed before any tidings were received, her anxiety had been hardly less than that of Nelson himself . . . and when the tidings were brought her by a joyful bearer open-mouthed, its effect was such, that she fell like one who had been shot. She and Sir William had literally been made ill by their hopes and fears, and joy at a catastrophe so far exceeding all that they had dared to hope for. Their admiration for the hero necessarily produced a degree of proportionate gratitude and affection; and when their barge came alongside the Vanguard, at the sight of Nelson Lady Hamilton sprang up the ship's side, and exclaiming, O God! is it possible! fell into his arms,— more, he says, like one dead than alive (2, 7–8).

Finally, when he feels that he must make a definitive statement on the relationship, Southey misrepresents. "It is certain that he had now formed an infatuated attachment for Lady Hamilton, which totally weaned his affections from his wife. Farther than this, there is no reason to believe that this most unfortunate attachment was criminal:—but this was criminality enough, and it brought with it its punishment" (2, 42). The reader may be inclined to ponder a noncriminal infatuation which could wean a man's affections completely from his wife, but he is almost immediately distracted by the imputation that the power of this infatuation led Nelson to two decisions which permanently damaged his reputation: "To all other persons [than Nelson], it was obvious that he was influenced by an infatuated attachment,—a baneful passion, which destroyed his domestic happiness, and now, in a second instance, stained ineffaceably his public character" (2, 52). The reader's attention is swept past the "attachment" itself and its true nature into a consideration of its effects upon Nelson. Southey is determined to avoid scandal: he is just as determined to avoid having to lie more than once. His only misrepresentation of the true nature of the relationship is a brief phrase: "no reason to believe that this . . . was criminal." Having stated this as quickly and as concretely as possible, Southey moves on to draw his conclusions from an honest, realistic estimate of the affair. Never again does he deny that Emma was Nelson's mistress. When he comes to Nelson's codicil to his will and its mention of Horatia, Southey seeks refuge in an impersonal statement in the passive voice: "The child, of whom this writing speaks, was believed to be his daughter, and so, indeed, he called her the last time that he pronounced her name" (2, 245). At the crucial moment, when he must declare himself one way or the other, Southey suppresses the truth, but (although the entire book takes as little notice of Emma as possible) Southey's further discussion of her seems grounded in an honest estimate of Nelson's love.

Southey must have known the truth. The world seems to have known,[9] and Southey was not one to miss out on so significant a contemporary anecdote. But the fact had not been published, and to publish it would be to give credence to scandal. Nelson's letters to Emma were brought out the year after Southey's *Nelson* appeared, but in none of his several revisions of the book between 1814 and 1830 did he change his statements con-

---

9. See above, Chapter Three, pp. 53–58, and references cited there.

cerning Emma or his public verdict on the matter. Emma died in 1815, but Horatia still lived. The feelings of the living were the only excuse for suppression; besides, except for a very brief lie, Southey told the truth.

This book seems much too easy, too facile, too readily written to be seriously considered the masterpiece of short biography it is. Southey himself fostered the impression of ease by rather offhand references to its composition in his correspondence. He refers to it as "my Life of Nelson, a subject not self-chosen—and out of my way, but executed *con amore.*"[1] In another letter he not only implies that the book was written to order (or rather to boil a pot) but emphasizes its technical difficulty—artistic conception is not mentioned.

> This is a subject which I should never have dreamt of touching, if it had not been thrust upon me. I have walked among sea terms as carefully as a cat does among crockery; but, if I have succeeded in making the narrative continuous and clear—the very reverse of what it is in the lives before me—the materials are, in themselves, so full of character, so picturesque, and so sublime, that it cannot fail of being a good book.[2]

In this statement he seems almost to abdicate artistic responsibility and give all credit to the strength of the material, a view of biography which he criticized in others.

The structure of the book belies such indifference. Every excerpted letter, every anecdote, supports Southey's image of Nelson. Every description, every narrated event, every one of Southey's own observations works into his plan for the book.

The plan must have grown out of Nelson's brief statement which appeared in both the review and the finished life. It is Nelson's dark night of the soul.

---

1. Letter to Sir Walter Scott, 13 Jan. 1813 (*Life and Correspondence*, 1849–50, *4*, 9).
2. Letter to the Rev. Robert Hill, 1 Feb. 1813 (ibid., *4*, 17).

"I felt impressed," said he, "with a feeling that I should never rise in my profession. My mind was staggered with a view of the difficulties I had to surmount, and the little interest I possessed. I could discover no means of reaching the object of my ambition. After a long and gloomy reverie, in which I almost wished myself overboard, a sudden glow of patriotism was kindled within me, and presented my king and country as my patron. 'Well, then,' I exclaimed, 'I will be a hero! and, confiding in Providence, I will brave every danger!' " Long afterwards Nelson loved to speak of the feeling of that moment: and from that time, he often said, a radiant orb was suspended in his mind's eye, which urged him onward to renown. The state of mind in which these feelings began, is what the mystics mean by their season of darkness, or aridity, and of desertion. If the animal spirits of coarser enthusiasts fail, they represent it as an actual temptation, a snare of Satan. The enthusiasm of Nelson's nature had taken a different direction, but in its essence it was the same. He knew to what the previous state of dejection was to be attributed; that an enfeebled body, and a mind depressed, had cast this shade over his soul: but he always seemed willing to believe, that the sunshine which succeeded bore with it a prophetic glory, and that the light which led him on, was "light from heaven" (*1, 24–25*).

That "radiant orb" is the organizing principle of Southey's *Nelson*. From it radiate all the quirks, frustrations, failings, and victories of the subject. Oversimplified, it is Nelson's egotism, or his heroism, sense of conviction, or superego. It is the mark at which Southey constantly aims, even though he (or Nelson) calls it heroism, or honor, or patriotism, or simple justice. The young Nelson is following the orb over the ice, chasing the bear, ignoring his officer's signal to return, even as the mature Nelson follows it at Copenhagen, long-glass set firmly to his blind eye. Every action presented in anecdote proceeds from this principle, every statement excerpted from the letters enforces it.

93

Connected with this central conception is a series of leitmotifs which runs through the book, testing the central conception, amplifying it, or enlarging upon it. The first of these is familiar to every common reader of biography as a rather hoary convention: the close call with a bud-nipping fate. For Nelson, such narrow escapes are plentiful: the "monitory lizard" at San Bartolomeo, dysentery at San Juan, the continual threats to resign his commission (*1*, 35, 38, 74, 83, and passim). This is not an original device with Southey, but he lifts it beyond convention by connecting it with Nelson's inner conviction—his radiant orb. The "battle" is drawn up between Nelson's devotion to this sense of destiny and the various threats to the fulfillment of destiny (lawsuits, conventions, commanding officers, lack of recognition). Each close call is a minor climax in the battle. They cannot, perhaps, be said to keep the reader in suspense or even in any real anxiety, but in conjunction with the other themes in the structure of the book, they produce a rhythm of tension, and enforce the lively animation of Southey's narrative.

Another tension, the "infatuation" with Lady Hamilton, is by implication involved in the first. Love, as it confronts heroism, fills Southey with a sense of foreboding. Every time a woman is mentioned, a prediction of dire consequences follows.

Nelson took [Alexander Davison's] . . . arm, to walk towards the town, and told him he found it utterly impossible to leave Quebec without again seeing the woman whose society had contributed so much to his happiness there, and offering her his hand.—"If you do," said his friend, "your utter ruin must inevitably follow."—"Then let it follow," cried Nelson, "for I am resolved to do it."—"And I," replied Davison, "am resolved you shall not." Nelson, however, upon this occasion was less resolute than his friend, and suffered himself to be led back to the boat (*1*, 44–45).

Emma enters to the strains of Southey's most woeful predictions; he is convinced that Nelson's infatuation was the cause of his only dishonor—the only time he was distracted from his "orb."[3] Southey constructs around this conviction an elaborate conflict, culminating in the Naples incidents, Nelson's only "blot." Southey's conflict, and the series of forebodings—his continual interpretation of women as a destructive, distracting element—support his explanation for an irregularity that will not fit into his conception of his hero. The only possible explanation must be that his hero was not at those moments true to his own "radiant orb," that he was not then really himself.

Another leitmotif of the book emanates from the central conflict between death and fulfillment of destiny, but this represents not so much Southey's interpretation of his materials as it does an organization of something which continually preyed on Nelson's mind: his own preoccupation with death and his fear of fate. Nelson's consciousness of this is manifested in his cries of "Westminster Abbey, or victory!" (*1,* 173) and his continual reference to the cypresses of death. Before practically every encounter he has a premonition that he will not return from it (*1,* 223, *2,* 122). This is perhaps just a reflection of Nelson's obsession with honor, but Southey attaches even greater significance to it. He introduces a physical representation of the feeling: the coffin made from the mainmast of *L'Orient* presented to Nelson by Captain Hallowell. Southey plays all the changes on this piece of furniture as effectively (or with as heavy a hand) as Richardson plays upon Clarissa Harlowe's coffin. Just after the presentation, Southey identifies the coffin as a physical representation of Nelson's consciousness of death.

> An offering so strange, and yet so suited to the occasion, was received by Nelson in the spirit with which it was sent. As if he felt it good for him, now that he was at the summit of his wishes, to have death before his eyes, he ordered the coffin to be placed upright in his cabin. Such a piece of furniture, however, was more suitable to his own feelings than to those of his guests and attendants; and an old favourite servant

3. Violation of a flag of truce and execution of a patriot, Francesco Caraccioli (2, 43-46, 50-53).

entreated him so earnestly to let it be removed, that at length he consented to have the coffin carried below (*1*, 238–39).

Southey underlines the thematic importance of the coffin by repeating the anecdote later in different terms. In its second appearance, the coffin provides a stark introduction to the Neapolitan controversy, a series of incidents which seems irrational to Southey. The coffin becomes a manifestation of Nelson's irrationality, the twisting of his mind produced by Emma's powers of distraction.

It was just at this time that he received from Capt. Hallowell the present of the coffin. Such a present was regarded by the men with natural astonishment: one of his old shipmates in the Agamemnon said—"We shall have hot work of it indeed! You see the admiral intends to fight till he is killed; and there he is to be buried." Nelson placed it upright, against the bulkhead of his cabin, behind his chair where he sat at dinner. The gift suited him at this time. It is said that he was disappointed in the son-in-law whom he had loved so dearly from his childhood, and who had saved his life at Teneriffe: and it is certain that he had now formed an infatuated attachment for Lady Hamilton, which totally weaned his affections from his wife (2, 42).

No mention is made here that the coffin is an honorable trophy of war, a relic of one of Nelson's greatest victories. Southey now wishes us to see it not as a trophy "fitting the occasion," but an emblem of Nelson's state of mind—it "suited him at the time." Lady Hamilton's influence is the valley of the shadow; the coffin, now with its dark side turned toward us, becomes a fit introduction to that descent into irrationality, a token of his distraction from the "orb" of honor. It is not introduced as allegory—it is not that precisely defined—but several possibilities of interpretation are opened. Southey introduces the anecdote as if it had just occurred to him: "It was about this time." He seems not to have thought it through, or to have intended a specifically limited meaning for the coffin, but it organizes a pattern which he sees throughout Nelson's life. It unites two conflicts or tensions; here the threat of death and the threat of love coincide. Southey feels this is strange, and somehow meaningful, so he underlines the coincidence, even sacrificing his ideal of brevity by repeating an anecdote he has already used.

A third central conflict is drawn up: Nelson's opposition to the conventions of society. The "ungrateful nation," a traditional antagonist in the life of a military hero, is the basic framework for the conflict. It is the background for all Nelson's actions, the obstacle to his victories, and the arbiter of his insufficient rewards. The ungrateful nation is represented as the norm of accustomed human mores and conventions: the world of little men, petty rules, and shortsighted decisions which Nelson must overcome that he may remain true to his "radiant orb" of honor. It is a bureaucracy which asks the hero for a medical certificate for his blind eye, the court which pursues Nelson with legal claims brought against him for enforcing British law; its sense of honor is a grudging recognition of his victories by a style of dignity always two or three levels below what he deserves. It rewards other men willing to work within its framework, but withholds recognition from Nelson because he is not.

The most skillful definition of this theme comes after the battle of the Nile. "Nelson was now at the summit of his glory," says Southey. But he proceeds to catalogue not the British rewards or laurels, but foreign recognition: a pelisse of sables, a diamond aigrette, and a handsome purse from the Turks; jeweled tokens from the Czar, the King of Sardinia, the court at Naples. "In his own country the king granted these honourable augmentations to his armorial ensign" (*I*, 242–44). A stiff, legal chill sets in as Southey recites the augmentation in the language of the Herald's Office. His pension is of two thousand pounds "for his own life, and those of his two immediate successors." In Commons, Pitt answers General Walpole's questioning of the stinginess of a barony for the hero of the Nile, by remarking that "he thought it needless to enter into that question. 'Admiral Nelson's fame,' he said, 'would be coequal with the British name, and it would be remembered that he had obtained the greatest naval victory on record: when no man would think of asking, Whether he had been created a baron, a viscount, or an earl?' " (*1*, 245). This was the final irony: in order to excuse a lower dignity, the minister had to argue England's inability ever to award an honor consistent with the glory Nelson had brought to his nation.

All three leitmotifs support the central conception of Nelson as a man obsessed and possessed with a drive toward a goal not of this world. He meets all his frustrations and setbacks with expressions of dismay or astonishment that the rest of the world cannot hear his voices, or glimpse his "radiant orb" or at least recognize his right to a greater impulse. All three conflicts or leitmotifs meet in a quiet scene in the garden at Merton. Nelson has retired, satisfied with his own sense of fulfillment of his destiny, at least grudgingly recognized by an otherwise ungrateful nation. The combined fleets are forming; Nelson hears of it from Blackwood and becomes momentarily excited, but is distracted by thought of the women. "When Blackwood had left him, he wanted a resolution to declare his wishes to Lady Hamilton and his sisters, and endeavoured to drive away the thought.—He had done enough; he said,—'let the man trudge it who has lost his budget!' " (2, 226–27). His lack of resolution results from giving in momentarily to two antagonists: the women and love, and the realization that he will not be properly rewarded by his nation. Emma enters—a dark figure for Southey up to this point. In recognition of what he must feel to be a basic change in her nature, the biographer permits her to speak in her own voice, for the first and only time in the book. Nelson replies with his famous apophthegm: "Brave Emma!—Good Emma!—If there were more Emmas, there would be more Nelsons" (2, 228). Southey seems to have resolved all his conflicts at once.

There remains but the final, inevitable victory and death.

They are regarded so by Nelson, they are so treated by Southey. The final chapter becomes a prolonged but animated narrative of Nelson's search for death. Southey dwells upon Nelson's conviction that he will be killed, and brings in all the participants and stage trappings of the death scene long before the death itself. The French snipers are in the rigging, the Admiral has donned all his identifying decorations. The theme of death is resolved in the garden at Merton, too; all that follows is the enactment of a carefully prepared scene.

The treatment of the scene in the garden need only be compared to any succeeding version as it has attempted to amplify Southey's conciseness. It stands, with a few others (Cavendish's description of Wolsey's interview in the great window with Henry VIII, Roper's depiction of Thomas More's last interview with his wife) as a master's achievement of the summit of biographical animation. Stanfield's concept of "character . . . at a single stroke"[4] could have been written to describe such rare dramatic moments.

Southey makes several allusions to mystics, saints, and martyrs. The parallel is not accidental, but neither is it developed too overtly. Overemphasized, this particular theme might appear to be only a repetition of the saintly conventions of pietistic exemplary lives. That the parallel was intended, however, seems inescapable, because of the timing of the allusions. Nelson's early depression (from which he emerged with the ideal of the "radiant orb") is equated with the mystics' "season of darkness." After his death, Nelson's lead coffin and the burial ensign are torn to pieces for relics. Southey's final peroration strongly underlines the parallel: "The most triumphant death is that of the martyr; the most awful, that of the martyred patriot; the most splendid, that of the hero in the hour of victory: and if the chariot and the horses of fire had been vouchsafed for Nelson's translation, he could scarcely have departed in a brighter blaze of glory" (2, 274–75). Nelson's final resolution and determined journey to meet death are narrated by Southey

4. See above, Chapter Four, pp. 69–70.

as a well rehearsed, mythic succession of events which take on an almost ritualistic tempo. This, together with the religious allusions, Nelson's lifelong obsession with death, and his fanatic devotion to a "radiant orb" of another world, give Southey's *Nelson* all the best qualities of hagiography, without the distortion and dehumanization which characterize its worst side. Southey approaches Nelson with the respectful puzzlement, the legendary tone, and the wholehearted belief in his subject which characterize some of the better lives of some of the more difficult saints. He attempts to explain in human terms the strange behavior of a man who heard voices, to explain to an ungrateful nation its national saint's irregularities.

As implied earlier, the "example" which Southey avows in his opening and closing words arises from the contemporary climate which fostered exemplary biography, but under Southey's hand the example presented in *Nelson* is of a different metal, a different mold, and achieves a different effect. He does not offer the reader a portrait which might please his subject's relatives. It is not an example of impossible, inhuman piety which was the uniform product of so much of nineteenth-century exemplary biography. Rather it is the example of the man himself: an attempt to weld the difficult quirks, frustrations, convictions, and limitations of the man's personality to the known body of the hero's measurable public achievements. It is an attempt to present the whole of a man who heeded a different drummer, who formed his life upon rules and conditions of a nonworldly ideal, but who still spoke the language of men, had a powerful hold upon men, experienced human frustration, bitterness, and the adversity of a world which neither recognized his ideal nor properly rewarded his achievements. The conventional exemplary life washed out humanity, personality, and irregularities for the sake of a uniform piety. Southey emphasizes Nelson's human peculiarities—the insubordination, resentment of all authority, obsession with death and with his "ungrateful nation"—in order to amplify the deeds of Nelson. The victories and the public character were testimony enough of greatness to support a penetrating examination of his less appealing personality. Southey succeeded, somehow, in satisfying Virginia Woolf's impossible criterion: he joined the granite of fact to the rainbow of personality.[5]

5. "If we think of truth as something of granite-like solidity and of personality as something of rainbow-like intangibility and reflect that the aim of biography is to weld these two into one seamless whole, we shall admit that the problem is a stiff one and that we need not wonder if biographers have for the most part failed to solve it" ("The New Biography," in *Granite and Rainbow*, 1958, p. 149).

CHAPTER SIX

MOORE'S BYRON: MYTH IN A MOLD

> What helps it now, that Byron bore,
> With haughty scorn which mock'd the smart,
> Through Europe to the Aetolian shore
> The pageant of his bleeding heart?
>
> —MATTHEW ARNOLD,
> "Stanzas from the Grande Chartreuse"

Surely Byron was the subject who had everything: noble birth, inner torment, immense popularity, perhaps the most poetic death since Sir Philip Sidney. That there was no biography which realized this potential is not explained away by reference to the exemplary principle, biographical dignity, or family reticence. Each of these contributes to the problem, but no combination of them produces a fully satisfactory solution.

In hindsight, it seems that a life of Byron could have combined all the most exciting and popular elements of the age into a dazzling compound: an ancestry out of *Waverley*, true romance (as well as truly sensational scandal), travels enough for the most travel-minded reader, the table talk of a wit, and the death of an idealist, if not of a hero. Yet when the time came to collect these raw materials, there was no creative synthesis, but only deadening fragmentation. Kennedy, Medwin, and Lady Blessington took the table talk, Blaquière, Gamba, and Pinto took the travels, many hands combined to dull the ancestry, and Parry took the death. Attempts at combination were a transparently pirated pastiche (the 1825 anonymous *Life, Writings, Opinions*), and a sprawling, unselective conglomeration by Thomas Moore. The contemporary assumption that the subject was the author of his life, or that biography writes itself, was never more emphatically refuted. Simple, undisguised prudery was one force which positively limited the biographers. For once, the self-appointed guardians of collective conscience were not battling with a straw man when they feared the revelation of damaging immorality: Byron had it in him, and everybody knew it. But if a biographer averted his eyes from these moral infirmities, he might also very well lose track of the man who was so much a creature of his weaknesses. Reticence was damaging, but reticence was not all.

A more serious threat to a formed, unified treatment of Byron's life was the existence of a firmly established body of illusory narratives which had obscured and distorted his real experiences. Some he had created himself: the heightened torment of *Childe Harold,* the obscure past of *The Corsair,* the ironic disguises of *Don Juan*—all had bits of the real Byron adhering to them here and there, insufficiently covered by layers of fictional gloom, incident, or pose. And not all of these fictional adventures saw print: Byron at table in his cups could apparently improvise reminiscences with as great ease as his poems slyly transformed them. Even the much lamented, righteously burnt Memoirs (if the numerous "recollections" of them can be believed) might reveal only a more ordered version of the epistolary, *Random Thoughts,* table wit Byron. His emphasis, even in describing them to Moore, is on their powers of entertainment, rather than their revelatory value. The epistolary Byron was no less a distortion of self in its ironic despairs and fictive exultations. The people and places revealed in letters were certainly more to be relied upon, but the emotions underwent a final protective disguise of bravado or melancholy before being sent off to his friends. Wordsworth's caution about the biographical fraud of letters was well taken in Byron.

Self-distortions were doubled and trebled through the process of rumor, both verbal and printed. The anecdote was never more valued than in the early nineteenth century, and with his sudden fame, Byron anecdotes were coin of the realm. Lady Caroline Lamb did her part in *Glenarvon,* and even Southey's appointment of Byron to command the Satanic School must have had a positive effect upon the poet's popular image—more an effect of dark fascination than of righteous recoil.

The biographer taking up the gage, then, was obliged not only to order, and to reveal, but to reorder, refute, and set straight—to destroy or realign the myth before proceeding to construct his image of the man. In so destroying or so naturalizing myth, some damage to legitimate issues of Byron's life would be inevitable. Not only was some of the Byron myth more attractive than the reality, it was more relevant than the corresponding facts which the earnest biographer felt obliged to give his readers. Indeed, Byron's whole construction of a fictive life, his transformation of a bored and dissolute wandering about Europe into the journey haunted by a dark melancholy is perhaps the most significant single thread of organization upon which a powerful biography might have been strung. We are more aware of the mask because of the current empery of psychology, but Southey's structural base—Nelson's fixation upon his orb of honor—was not more tangible in 1813 than what strikes us today as the core of Byron's biography.

It is, of course, fruitless to speculate upon the possibilities of a life written upon an unrecognized plan. Perhaps more to the point is a detailed examination of the grandest failure of the lot: Thomas Moore's *Byron*—grandest because of its attempt, its potential, its scope; a failure for the same reasons.

The contemporary critics were predisposed in Moore's favor: he had selflessly consented to the burning of the Memoirs and had the most clear-cut right to comment upon Byron. Then, too, the critics were so relieved that Moore had not produced a handbook of vice for the library tables of their nieces, daughters, and aunts that they elevated his skill at equivocation and his asterisked reserve to the level of literary art. Even today, we *want* to like Moore's book, but no matter how we explain away this or that, no matter how it is excerpted, cited, or read, it remains an unsatisfactory and unwieldy scrapbook; even the faint light of Byron's personality which manages to break through the mass of undigested, unrealized material is not brought forth by Moore's forming hand but comes through in spite of it. What appeals in the book is fragmented autobiography, not the scheme or vision or control of biography. Moore's failure was not predestined. It was made inevitable by a series of personal semi-artistic decisions he made when confronted with a wealth of material, his predecessors in Byroniana, his responsibilities, and his image of Byron.

Each of the three major literary functions or responsibilities of the biographer—selection, form and design, and an organizing principle—was known and valued by Moore, but each was finally abdicated in an unsatisfactory personal rationalization. He was an experienced biographer: his *Life of Richard Brinsley Sheridan* was in preparation at the time of Byron's death,[1] and he had been thinking about turning his Byron papers to profit long before the Sheridan project came up. But somehow he could never reach a properly objective professional approach to Byron's life. To the first request from Rees (of the Longmans firm) to urge his "immediate application to Lord Byron's family, and to all other sources likely to furnish them, for materials towards my intended 'Memoirs of Byron.' Answered that I would do so, as soon as the funeral was over, but that it would be indecorous till then. Looked over the Journals, &c. I have of Byron's, and find much in them that may be made use of."[2] He knew he had an advantage in his collection of papers, and in his friendship with other possessors of papers and correspondence. He knew he was uniquely fitted to the task by experience, familiarity, and discretion: "It was always his own wish that I should . . . write something about him, and . . . I thought it must be equally now the wish of his family that a hand, upon whose delicacy they could rely, should undertake

1. It was published in Oct. 1825; Moore had contracted with Murray for it before he left England in 1819, but did not begin work on it in earnest until 1823. (Thomas Moore, *Memoirs, Journal, and Correspondence*, ed. Lord John Russell, 8 vols. 1853–56, *3*, 166; *4*, passim).

2. 19–30 June 1824, ibid., *4*, 209.

the task, rather than have his memory at the mercy of scribblers, who dishonour alike the living and the dead."[3] It was just these scribblers who complicated Moore's venture. Each new volume of reminiscences, travels, and other Byroniana multiplied distortions which would have to be corrected, and which made his task more difficult: "Though the Longmans look earnestly and anxiously to it as the great source of my means of repaying them their money; and though it would be the shortest and easiest way I could effect that object; yet the subject begins to be so tarnished and clogged with difficulties, that my *own* impression is that I *ought* not to undertake it."[4]

At first he felt that a way out would be to restrict himself to "a critical examination of his works and genius."[5] Later he tended to Hobhouse's solution: "enough of original matter of Byron might be collected to make up a volume of such a size as would spare me the trouble of doing more than merely prefixing a light prefatory sketch to it."[6] His decision in November 1827 was a compromise based on this solution: "Have resolved not to attempt a regular biography, but to call it 'Letters and Journals of Lord Byron, with Biographical Illustrations (or Notices of his Life), by T. M.' "[7]

Moore feared association with those who had parlayed an

3. 19 Nov. 1824, ibid., *4*, 252.

4. 22 Nov. 1824, ibid., *4*, 253. In the midst of his private soul-searching Moore was always careful to preserve the appearance of the official biographer: "It is my intention . . . to leave both the Longmans and the public under the impression that I *do* mean to write the life" (ibid.). At one point during the off-again on-again negotiations with John Murray for *his* papers (ibid., *5*, 77, 97, 110, 154), Murray thought that Moore was offering to give up his documents. Moore explained "that, as to parting with a paper of Lord Byron's (except to put it in the fire) there was nothing more remote from my thoughts" (ibid., *5*, 155, 26 Feb. 1827). He seems always to have intended the project, and the agonizing self-argument concerned only what form his Byron book was to take and the best time for springing it on the public.

5. Ibid., *4*, 253.

6. 3 July 1827, ibid., *5*, 185.

7. 17–19 Nov. 1827, ibid., *5*, 238–39.

acquaintance or a shipboard friendship with the poet into a profit. But he was already grouped with this sort: everyone assumed that he was in it for the money because so much had already been made of his "investment" in the Memoirs at their burning (an argument often advanced by himself and others). Perhaps more compelling, however, the destruction of the Memoirs had laid a peculiar burden of justification upon him. Shortly after the burning, and frequently thereafter, Moore asserted that no significant information had been lost in the destruction that was unobtainable elsewhere, thus challenging himself to produce it from "elsewhere."

This was only part of a formidable challenge which his non-biography had to meet. He had to give the lie to previously published Byroniana, for he was the guardian of the last word, both by virtue of his erstwhile possession of the Memoirs and his considerable body of Byron papers. So many false impressions required so many documents: his life would be the best by sheer force of inclusion.

If Moore was to court inclusion, he had to abandon selectivity. His conscience seems to have been troubled only slightly, and for the wrong reason—he had some doubts about biographical dignity.

Already, indeed, I may be thought by some readers to have occupied too large a portion of these pages, not only in tracing out such "nice dependencies" and gradations of my friend's character, but still more uselessly, as may be conceived, in recording all the various habitudes and whims by which the course of his every-day life was distinguished from that of other people. That the critics of the day should think it due to their own importance to object to trifles is naturally to be expected; but that in other times, such minute records of a Byron will be read with interest, even such critics cannot doubt.[8]

8. Thomas Moore, *Letters and Journals of Lord Byron: with Notices of His Life* (2 vols. John Murray, 1830), 2, 797–98. Further references to this work appear in parentheses in the text.

Such accumulation adds interest, but it destroys literary effect, as Southey so clearly pointed out and so brilliantly demonstrated. An all-inclusive principle would by sheer volume also cover the traces of whatever suppression he felt he had to make in the name of decency. Inclusion of Byron's every decent word all but precluded the possibility of a first-rate biography.

The principles behind the hand of suppression "upon whose delicacy the family could rely" was not that of a common prude (although perhaps that of an uncommon one). He had learned from public reaction at the time of the Memoir burning[9] that there was a precarious balance to maintain. He must attempt to dissociate himself from the "scribblers" who turned acquaintance to profit, but, more important, he could not appear to surrender to the contemporary cant of decency and example. Commentators of this cast had done violence to Byron while he was alive, and Moore, by inclination and by choice, was determined to defend Byron's claim to a reputation unprejudiced by moral judgments. The family supplied the papers, so their wishes would have to be respected. Scribblers had told lies and distorted the truth: if he could, with decency, tell a truth which would refute a lie or correct a distortion, he would do so. Or if he could give a fact which would refute an anecdote of the Byron myth (either one of Byron's own, or one fostered by the public) he would.

Moore's asterisks (thanks to G. Wilson Knight and others) are all too famous for us to regard his practice of suppression without bias. Moore's reputation as self-righteous censor is not altogether just. He was determined to avoid giving pain to Byron's survivors, friend and enemy alike, so he felt he had to avoid even surmise on dark chapters of Byron's career: "To mere opinions I am not called upon to pay attention—and, still less, to insinuations or mysteries" (2, 807). He omitted names of the living, but in varying degrees ("***" and at one point "Lady C. L**" for Lady Caroline Lamb, and "C————e"

---

9. See Chapter 3, above, and references there cited, especially *Monthly Review*, III, *13* (1830), 218.

for Coleridge) (*1*, 357, 356, 316).[1] Asterisks in the texts of letters covered a multitude of indiscretions, from Byron's mild praise for William Beckford[2] to more understandable (if no more excusable) excision of the Fornarina's extreme religious zeal.[3] Certain relationships were distorted silently (that is, without even the sanction of asterisk): Claire Clairmont is mentioned only in passing reference to Shelley and his wife ("a female relative of the latter" 2, 22), but the foreign mistresses received at his hands almost candid recognition (in the Moore scale at least).

A when-in-Rome principle provided a sliding scale of value. Discretion was an English standard. He was determined, when writing about Europeans, to do as they did.

. . . Without leaving altogether unnoticed (what, indeed, was too notorious to be so evaded) certain affairs of gallantry in which he had the reputation of being engaged, I have thought it right . . . to suppress also whatever passages in his Journals and Letters might be supposed to bear too personally or particularly on the same delicate topics. Incomplete as the strange history of his mind and heart must, in one of its most interesting chapters, be left by these omissions, still a deference to that peculiar sense of decorum in this country, which marks the mention of such frailties as hardly a less crime than the commission of them, and, still more, the regard due to the feelings of the living, who ought not rashly to be made to suffer for the errors of the dead, have combined to render this sacrifice, however much it may be regretted, necessary.

1. Cf. Marchand, *Byron* (1957), *1*, 350.

2. "The first and sweetest spot in this kingdom is Montserrat, lately the seat of the great Beckford," letter to Francis Hodgson, 16 July 1809. Marchand (*1*, 187) quotes the deleted passage.

3. "She was very devout, and would cross herself if she heard the prayer-time strike [—sometimes when that ceremony did not appear to be much in unison with what she was then about]." Moore omits the bracketed passage (2, 188); supplied by Marchand, 2, 756.

We have now, however, shifted the scene to a region where less caution is requisite;—where, from the different standard applied to female morals in these respects, if the wrong itself be not lessened by this diminution of the consciousness of it, less scruple may be, at least, felt towards persons so circumstanced, and whatever delicacy we may think right to exercise in speaking of their frailties must be with reference rather to our views and usages than theirs (2, 51).

Having entered his disclaimer to the prevailing moral climate, Moore announces he will include "with but little suppression, the noble poet's letters relative to his Italian adventures" (ibid.). That is, he will call a whore a whore, but will omit bedroom scenes.

To throw a veil altogether over these irregularities of his private life would be to afford—were it even practicable—but a partial portraiture of his character; while, on the other hand, to rob him of the advantage of being himself the historian of his errors (where no injury to others can flow from the disclosure) would be to deprive him of whatever softening light can be thrown round such transgressions by the vivacity and fancy, the passionate love of beauty, and the strong yearning after affection which will be found to have, more or less, mingled with even the least refined of his attachments (2, 51–52).

"No injury to others" apparently applies only to English "others"; the skeptic might also feel that Moore was excusing moral transgressions only insofar as the transgressor was capable of a skillful or clever narration of it.

Even this sliding scale, however, does not hold throughout the book. The domestic qualities of the Guiccioli liaison apparently seem to have caught Moore off guard. The relationship had in it "all of marriage that his real marriage wanted," and Moore gradually softened the edges of "transgression" with sentiment and a peculiar equivocation: "What a change for a young and simple girl, who, but a few weeks before, had thought only of society and the world, but who now saw no other happiness but in the hope of becoming worthy, by seclusion and self-instruction, of the illustrious object of her love!" (2, 212). By virtue of her domesticity, Guiccioli eventually qualified herself for Moore's English standards of discretion. Apparently her feelings became more significant (or more English) as the liaison progressed, for finally Moore felt her worthy of full-scale English suppression.

> The impression which, I think, cannot but be entertained, from some passages of these letters, of the real fervour and sincerity of his attachment to Madame Guiccioli, would be still further confirmed by the perusal of his letters to that lady herself, both from Venice and during his present stay at Ravenna—all bearing, throughout, the true marks both of affection and passion. Such effusions, however, are but little suited to the general eye. It is the tendency of all strong feeling, from dwelling constantly on the same idea, to be monotonous; and those often repeated vows and verbal endearments, which make the charm of true love-letters to the parties concerned in them, must for ever render even the best of them cloying to others (2, 226–27).

No amount of detailed reference to auction receipts, publishers' contracts, or diet regimen is correspondingly monotonous. It is a peculiar moment for Moore suddenly to become selective.

Evidently Moore's determination to comment as little as possible in the course of his book weakened rather early in its composition, and had more or less disappeared by its completion. His comments, for the most part, appeared as islands in a sea of correspondence and journals. When he came to a crisis, a poem, or a turning point in Byron's career he would pause to assess, reflect, or synthesize. Moore evidently did not conceive of these islands as a function of continuity or unity—something to fill documentary gaps or to explain with objective sequence the progress of subjective narration. He had a high aim for these passages, although they made up but a small portion of his book. They were to order and organize the portrait of Byron, to replace the biographer's organized selectivity by occasional interpretation of Byron's life as a whole.

Moore had, early in the book, rejected the eighteenth-century concept of the ruling passion "as insufficient and too restricting for an understanding of Byron." He adopted instead a stereotype theory of genius—every bit as restricting and insufficient —for his organizing principle. The broad outline is simple.

During the lifetime of a man of genius, the world is but too much inclined to judge of him rather by what he wants than by what he possesses, and even where conscious, as in the present case, that his defects are among the sources of his greatness, to require of him unreasonably the one without the other. If Pope had not been splenetic and irritable, we should have wanted his Satires; and an impetuous temperament, and passions untamed, were indispensable to the conformation of a poet like Byron. It is by posterity only that full justice is rendered to those who have paid such hard penalties to reach it. The dross that had once hung about the ore drops away, and the infirmities, and even miseries, of genius are forgotten in its greatness. Who now asks whether Dante was right or wrong in his matrimonial differences? ... The utter unreasonableness of trying such a character by ordinary standards, or of expecting to find the materials of order and happiness in a bosom constantly heaving forth from its depths such "lava floods," is—now that his spirit has passed from among us—felt and acknowledged (*1, 656*).

Defects are a necessary part (nay, the source) of greatness. Moore may proclaim Byron's genius and at the same time admit his failings, since they but support or prove genius. The tenor of the theory is uncomfortably close to Macaulay's theories on Boswell (his boorishness made him a great biographer), but the truth or falsity of the initial premises perhaps is not a legitimate concern for criticism of Moore's *Byron*.

For Byron's first visit to Missolonghi, Moore travels into the future on the heavy wings of rhetoric.

Could some Spirit have here revealed to him the events of
that interval,—have shown him, on the one side, the triumphs
that awaited him, the power his varied genius would acquire
over all hearts, alike to elevate or depress, to darken or
illuminate them,—and then place, on the other side, all the
penalties of this gift, the waste and wear of the heart through
the imagination, the havoc of that perpetual fire within,
which, while it dazzles others, consumes the possessor,—the
invidiousness of such an elevation in the eyes of mankind,
and the revenge they take on him who compels them to look
up to it,—*would* he, it may be asked, have welcomed glory
on such conditions? (*1*, 211).

This was not artificial enthusiasm. Moore believed in Byron,
and a curious combination of his personal experience with
the poet, private hero worship, and certainly no small measure
of the public Byron myth contributed to his selection of the
heroism of genius as the central theme of his work. This is not
merely stylistic rapture, but ecstasy of belief.

Lord Byron was not formed to be long-lived. Whether from
any hereditary defect in his organization . . . or from those
violent means he so early took to . . . reduce himself to thin-
ness. . . . When to all this we add the wasteful wear of spirits
and strength from the slow corrosion of sensibility, the warfare of the passions, and the workings of a mind that allowed
itself no sabbath, it is not to be wondered at that the vital
principle in him should so soon have burnt out. . . . To feed
the flame, the all absorbing flame, of his genius, the whole
powers of his nature, physical as well as moral, were sacrificed;
—to present that grand and costly conflagration to the world's
eyes, in which,

"Glittering, like a palace set on fire,
His glory, while it shone, but ruined him!" (2, 762).[4]

4. The quotation is from Beaumont and Fletcher.

Moore contends that genius is absolute. Like all heroes to the archetypal critic, all geniuses in this theory have the same biography. There are certain common accesses of power.

In looking back through the lives of the most illustrious poets,—the class of intellect in which the characteristic features of genius are, perhaps, most strongly marked,—we shall find that, with scarcely one exception, from Homer down to Lord Byron, they have been, in their several degrees, restless and solitary spirits, with minds wrapped up, like silk-worms, in their own tasks, either strangers, or rebels, to domestic ties, and bearing about with them a deposite [sic] for Posterity in their souls, to the jealous watching and enriching of which almost all other thoughts and considerations have been sacrificed (*1,* 591).

The defects of genius not only gave Moore justification for the defense of Byron's moral vagaries, but provided him with a solution to what must have been the most difficult paradox of Byron's life: by inverse proportion, the more he wasted himself and his energies, the better his poems became. "In fact, so far from the powers of his intellect being at all weakened or dissipated by these irregularities, he was, perhaps, at no time of his life, so actively in the full possession of all its energies" (2, 181).

To a certain extent, the theory of genius implied the necessity of a hostile world—something similar to Nelson's "ungrateful nation," but perhaps more closely related to Carlyle's "perennial Battle."[5] Moore makes only a brief point from this in his summation of the portrait: "We have seen, for instance, that wrongs and sufferings were, through life, the main sources of Byron's inspiration. Where the hoof of the critic struck, the fountain was first disclosed; and all the tramplings of the world afterwards but forced out the stream stronger and brighter" (2, 784). But facts brought the theory to confusion. Except for some receptions of his first volume, the critics were not too

5. See Chapter Four, above, and references.

unkind to Byron (the "trampling" ungrateful nation could perhaps be found in the moralists who criticized Byron's later life). Moore ultimately discovered that Byron made much more sense as a representative of his age than as an opponent:

> There are those who trace in the peculiar character of Lord Byron's genius strong features of relationship to the times in which he lived; who think that the great events which marked the close of the last century, by giving a new impulse to men's minds, by habituating them to the daring and the free, and allowing full vent to "the flash and outbreak of fiery spirits," had led naturally to the production of such a poet as Byron; and that he was, in short, as much the child and representative of the Revolution, in poesy, as another great man of the age, Napoleon, was in statesmanship and warfare. Without going the full length of this notion, it will, at least, be conceded, that the free loose which had been given to all the passions and energies of the human mind, in the great struggle of that period, together with the constant spectacle of such astounding vicissitudes as were passing, almost daily, on the theatre of the world, had created, in all minds, and in every walk of intellect, a taste for strong excitement, which the stimulants supplied from ordinary sources were insufficient to gratify;—that a tame deference to established authorities had fallen into disrepute, no less in literature than in politics, and that the poet who should breathe into his songs the fierce and passionate spirit of the age, and assert, untrammeled and unawed, the high dominion of genius, would be the most sure of an audience toned in sympathy with his strains (*1, 343*).

Moore's real trouble came when he attempted to fit all the details of Byron's life into the framework of his theory of genius. There was little difficulty in Byron's boyhood (before his realization of his high destiny). It was "a period of natural affections." It antedated his genius—"before Imagination had yet accustomed him to those glowing pictures, after gazing upon which all else appeared cold and colourless" (*1, 593*). This period included all the boyhood friendships of which the twentieth century has become so suspicious, but natural affection continued as a faded glory which Byron attempted to recover or recapture—almost in a Wordsworthian sense—for the rest of his life. It is never a part of his genius, but that human warmth denied to genius, or that which genius somehow sullies and is never able to recover. Affection recollected in tranquillity becomes the keystone of a structure which explains a multitude of sins. On "Thyrza":

> His schoolsports with the favourites of his boyhood, Wingfield and Tattersall,—his summer days with Long, and those evenings of music and romance, which he had dreamed away in the society of his adopted brother, Eddlestone,—all these recollections of the young and dead now came to mingle themselves in his mind with the image of her, who, though living, was, for him, as much lost as they, and diffused that general feeling of sadness and fondness through his soul, which found a vent in these poems (*1*, 303).[6]

Moore wanders, perhaps unknowingly, dangerously close to what now seems to be the truth about "Thyrza." Homosexuality would fit in the explanation just as well as the "recollections" which Moore substitutes for it. Again, Moore's analysis of Byron's "friendship" with Augusta is ambiguous.

> To the same cause, there is little doubt, his love for his sister owed much of its devotedness and fervour. In a mind sensitive and versatile as his, long habits of family intercourse might have estranged, or at least dulled, his natural affection for her;—but their separation, during youth, left this feeling fresh and untried. His very inexperience in such ties made the smile of a sister no less a novelty than a charm to him, and

6. See also *1*, 243–44: "During this period of his stay in Greece, we find him forming one of those extraordinary friendships,—if attachment to persons so inferior to himself can be called by that name,—of which I have already mentioned two or three instances in his younger days, and in which the pride of being a protector, and the pleasure of exciting gratitude, seem to have constituted to his mind the chief, pervading charm."

before the first gloss of this newly awakened sentiment had time to wear off, they were again separated, and for ever (*1*, 595).[7]

The early yearning for affection does not seem to be rung in ad hoc to explain away some difficult relationships. It is part and parcel of Moore's paradigm of Byron's progress. He saw "affectionateness" as the most ardent of Byron's qualities: the "unsuccessful love" that followed the "passionate enthusiasm" of his "boyish friendships" was "the agony . . . of this unsated desire, which . . . filled his poetry with the very soul of tenderness, lent the colouring of its light to even those unworthy ties which vanity or passion led him afterwards to form, and was the last aspiration of his fervid spirit in those stanzas written but a few months before his death" (*1*, 177).

Moore also comes closer to the truth of May Gray than his readers could ever have suspected.

> While thus prematurely broken into the pains of life [his "ill-fated attachment" to Mary Chaworth], a no less darkening effect was produced upon him by too early an initiation into its pleasures. That charm with which the fancy of youth invests an untried world was, in his case, soon dissipated. His passions had, at the very onset of their career, forestalled the future; and the blank void that followed was by himself considered as one of the causes of that melancholy, which now settled so deeply into his character (*1*, 182).

By playing upon melancholy almost as ruthlessly as Byron ever did, Moore has arrived at a conflict firm enough to use as a core for his myth. The conventional "ungrateful world" would not work. The inner world of the "cocoon" faces the world of common men. It is a conflict of imagination and reality, and intrusions of objects, affections, aims, and desires of the real world become the villains of the piece. Victory or achievement depends, not on overcoming obstacles or fighting

---

7. The inclusion of the phrase "long habits of family intercourse," by its very naïveté almost absolves Moore of any suspicion that he knew much more about Byron and Augusta than he included in his book.

the good fight, but on maintaining inviolable the cocoon, on being true to "the high, hazardous chances" of being great.

> From the moment of this initiation into the wonders of his own mind, a distaste for the realities of life began to grow upon him. Not even that intense craving after affection . . . could keep his ardour still alive in a pursuit whose results fell so short of his "imaginings;" and though . . . the combined warmth of his fancy and temperament was able to call up a feeling which to his eyes wore the semblance of love, it may be questioned whether his heart had ever much share in such passions, or whether, after his first launch into the boundless sea of imagination, he could ever have been brought back and fixed by any lasting attachment. Actual objects there were, in but too great number, who, as long as the illusion continued, kindled up his thoughts and were the themes of his song. But they were, after all, little more than mere dreams of the hour;—the qualities with which he invested them were almost all ideal, nor could have stood the test of a month's, or even week's, cohabitation. It was but the reflection of his own bright conceptions that he saw in each new object; and while persuading himself that they furnished the models of his heroines, he was, on the contrary, but fancying that he beheld his heroines in them (*1*, 593).

Affection, initiation, alienation are followed by a leap of faith: the transfer of the imaginative affection back to real objects, surrounding them with the "colouring" of the imaginative world so that they can seem to be a part of it. The example of Petrarch and Laura which Moore so often cites is well taken, since the pattern, if not the result, of his paradigm is Neo-Platonic. "Those images of ideal good and beauty that surround him in his musings soon accustom him to consider all that is beneath this high standard unworthy of his care; till, at length, . . . it too often happens that, . . . as he has refined and elevated his theory of all the social affections, he has unfitted himself for the practice of them" (*1*, 590).

The intrusion of reality provides Moore with a convenient

explanation for the failure of Byron's marriage, for his excesses at Venice, and for those of Byron's poems which Moore did not happen to like. It works best for the marriage; even the narrative seems to be conceived in terms of the opposing worlds of illusion and reality:

> In the same mood, he wandered about the grounds alone, till he was summoned for the ceremony, and joined, for the first time on that day, his bride and her family. He knelt down,—he repeated the words after the clergyman; but a mist was before his eyes,—his thoughts were elsewhere; and he was but awakened by the congratulations of the bystanders, to find that he was—married (*1*, 599–600).

The whole idea of marriage is anathema to the theoretical genius: domestic happiness is a function of the norm by which the genius is unjustly judged. Such required close participation in the real world almost inevitably runs against the grain, and unhappy marriage becomes a traditional defect of genius.

> I have already, in some observations on the general character of men of genius, endeavoured to point out those peculiarities, both in disposition and habitudes, by which, in the far greater number of instances, they have been found unfitted for domestic happiness. Of these defects (which are, as it were, the shadow that genius casts, and too generally, it is to be feared, in proportion to its stature,) Lord Byron could not, of course, fail to have inherited his share, in common with all the painfully gifted class to which he belonged (*1*, 649).

It was not just that Lady Byron was so irrevocably of the real world, not that Byron failed to transfer an imaginative aura to her, but that marriage itself was indissolubly bound to reality. Real itself, it dragged even more real concerns into his life.

> By his marriage, and its results, he was again brought back to some of those bitter realities of which his youth had had a foretaste. Pecuniary embarrassment,—that ordeal, of all others, the most trying to delicacy and high-mindedness—

now beset him with all the indignities that usually follow in its train; and he was thus rudely schooled into the advantages of *possessing* money, when he had hitherto thought but of the generous pleasure of *dispensing* it. . . . Those imaginary, or, at least, retrospective sorrows, in which he had once loved to indulge, and whose tendency it was, through the medium of his fancy, to soften and refine his heart, were now exchanged for a host of actual, ignoble vexations, which it was even more humiliating than painful to encounter. His misanthropy, instead of being, as heretofore, a vague and abstract feeling, without any object to light upon, and losing therefore its acrimony in diffusion, was now, by the hostility he came in contact with, condensed into individual enmities, and narrowed into personal resentments; and from the lofty, and, as it appeared to himself, philosophical luxury of hating mankind in the gross, he was now brought down to the self-humbling necessity of despising them in detail (2, 391–92).

Misanthropy is a function of genius as long as it remains general; but when it is applied to individuals, it becomes a distracting force of reality.

A similar formula is applied to Byron's poetry. The sphere of the imagination is the only truly poetic arena; when Byron's poems lost or descended from the imaginative ideal, they were no longer worthy of his genius.

The title under which both pieces[8] were immediately announced by various publishers, as "Poems by Lord Byron on his domestic circumstances," carried with it a sufficient exposure of the utter unfitness of such themes for rhyme. It is, indeed, only in those emotions and passions, of which imagination forms a predominant ingredient,—such as love, in its first dreams, before reality has come to imbody or dispel them, or sorrow, in its wane, when beginning to pass away from the heart into the fancy,—that poetry ought ever to be employed as an interpreter of feeling. For the expression of all those immediate affections and disquietudes that have

8. Two poems: "Fare Thee Well," and "A Sketch."

their root in the actual realities of life, the art of the poet, from the very circumstance of its being an art, as well as from the coloured form in which it is accustomed to transmit impressions, cannot be otherwise than a medium as false as it is feeble (*1*, 664–65).

There were some moral offenses which Moore could allow (Byron's youthful passions or the spleen of *English Bards and Scots Reviewers*) and others which he could not (Venice[9] and *Don Juan*). The former he fits into his scheme of imagination and the high, hazardous call to genius; the latter must, perforce, be of reality—that which the poet may conceive to be part of his dream of life, but which is really, Moore points out, irrevocably of this world.

It was at this time . . . that he conceived, and wrote some part of, his Poem of "Don Juan;"—and never did pages more faithfully and, in many respects, lamentably reflect every variety of feeling, and whim, and passion that, like the rack of autumn, swept across the author's mind in writing them. Nothing less, indeed, than that singular combination of attributes, which existed and were in full activity in his mind at this moment, could have suggested, or been capable of, the execution of such a work. The cool shrewdness of age with the vivacity and glowing temperament of youth,—the wit of a Voltaire, with the sensibility of a Rousseau,—the minute, practical knowledge of the man of society, with the abstract and self-contemplative spirit of the poet,—a susceptibility of all that is grandest and most affecting in human virtue, with a deep, withering experience of all that is most fatal to it,—the two extremes, in short, of man's mixed and inconsistent nature, now rankly smelling of earth, now breathing of heaven,—such was the strange assemblage of

9. "Another consequence of the spirit of defiance now roused in him, and one that tended, perhaps, even more fatally than any yet mentioned, to sully and, for a time, bring down to earth the romance of his character, was the course of life to which, outrunning even the licence of his youth, he abandoned himself at Venice" (2, 393).

contrary elements, all meeting together in the same mind, and all brought to bear, in turn, upon the same task, from which alone could have sprung this extraordinary Poem,—the most powerful and, in many respects, painful display of the versatility of genius that has ever been left for succeeding ages to wonder at and deplore (2, 189).

The satiric Byron must be anticlimax to the melancholy Byron, because the theory of genius dictates that self-disillusionment comes after the final step of genius into the pure serene of perfect imagination. Self-ridicule, especially, must tarnish and debase the "silk-worm" self-concentration, must attack the core of the grand illusion of the poems, because they must be based in realities of the poet's life.

It was, indeed, wholly beyond the power, even of an imagination like his, to go on investing with its own ideal glories a sentiment which,—more from daring and vanity than from any other impulse,—he had taken such pains to tarnish and debase in his own eyes. Accordingly, . . . he now degenerated into the wholly opposite and perverse error of depreciating and making light of what, intrinsically, he valued, and, as the reader has seen, throwing slight and mockery upon a tie in which it was evident some of the best feelings of his nature were wrapped up. That foe to all enthusiasm and romance, the habit of ridicule, had, in proportion as he exchanged the illusions for the realities of life, gained further empire over him; and how far it had, at this time, encroached upon the loftier and fairer regions of his mind may be seen in the pages of Don Juan,—that diversified arena, on which the two Genii, good and evil, that governed his thoughts, hold, with alternate triumph, their ever powerful combat (2, 393).

Moore's prefabricated formula for genius simply did not fit Byron. At some junctures he had to define events or circumstances of Byron's life in a peculiar way in order to use the theory for Byron's moral justification; at other points he had to do violence to the theory to make Byron fit. Once, discrepancies between Byron's life and the theory were so apparent that Moore simply stuck in the facts and retreated into the theory as fast as he could.

The circumstances under which Lord Byron now took leave of England were such as, in the case of any ordinary person, could not be considered otherwise than disastrous and humiliating. He had, in the course of one short year, gone through every variety of domestic misery. . . . Had he been of that class of unfeeling and self-satisfied natures from whose hard surface the reproaches of others fall pointless, he might have found in insensibility a sure refuge against reproach; but, on the contrary, the same sensitiveness that kept him so awake to the applauses of mankind rendered him, in a still more intense degree, alive to their censure. Even the strange, perverse pleasure which he felt in painting himself unamiably to the world did not prevent him from being both startled and pained when the world took him at his word; and, like a child in a mask before a looking-glass, the dark semblance which he had half in sport, put on, when reflected back upon him from the mirror of public opinion, shocked even himself. . . . But in him,—furnished as was his mind with reserves of strength, waiting to be called out,—the very intensity of the pressure brought relief by the proportionate reaction which it produced. Had his transgressions and frailties been visited with no more than their due portion of punishment, there can be little doubt that a very different result would have ensued. . . . It was, indeed, not without truth, said of him by Goëthe, that he was inspired by the Genius of Pain,—for, from the first to the last of his agitated career, every fresh recruitment of his faculties was imbibed from that bitter source. His chief incentive, when a boy, to distinction was, as we have seen, that mark of deformity on his person, by an acute sense of which he was first stung into the ambition of being great (2, 1–2).

Perhaps Moore only intended to humanize the genius—to take into account the Byron of the affectionate boyhood and to try to spread its influence throughout the life. Perhaps he was only attempting to soften somewhat the cold image of a completely self-centered genius. Whatever his intent, this is contradiction. Human affection is weakness in this context, a lapse from self-concentration, a penetration of the private world of the imagination by Philistine reality. Moore covers as best he can, and puts himself back on the track by making the conventional pain of rejection by the world the muse for further creation.

Later in the life Moore now and again seems to give up his organizing structure entirely. He clings to the germs and catchwords of the theory but is not able to make them work in harmony with the progress of genius. Contradiction is now beside the point. He uses elements and terms of the theory impressionistically, painting away with abandon.

A time [that covered by the diary of 1814] which may be considered, to use his own words, as "the most poetical part of his whole life,"—*not*, certainly, in what regarded the powers of his genius, to which every succeeding year added new force and range, but in all that may be said to constitute the poetry of character,—those fresh, unworldly feelings, of which, in spite of his early plunge into experience, he still retained the gloss, and that ennobling light of imagination, which, with all his professed scorn of mankind, still followed in the track of his affections, giving a lustre to every object on which they rested. There was, indeed, in his misanthropy, as in his sorrows, at that period, to the full as much of fancy as of reality; and even those gallantries and loves in which he at the same time entangled himself, partook equally, as I have endeavoured to show, of the same imaginative character (2, 390–91).

The theory failed and Moore failed. He seems to have known it by the time he came to the end of the book. The closing portrait is an amalgam of apologies and protestations of the difficulty of a life of Byron. There was first, he says, the lack of a single ruling passion on which the biographer could hang the vicissitudes of his life: no "one leading principle or passion consistent enough in its operations to be taken confidently into account in any estimate" (2, 782). Byron was too elusive, too changeable to conform to any such human expectation.

Governed as he was at different moments by totally different passions, and impelled sometimes . . . by springs of action never before developed in his nature, in him this simple mode of tracing character to its sources must be often wholly at fault; and if, as is not impossible, in trying to solve the strange variances of his mind, I should myself be found to have fallen into contradictions and inconsistencies, the extreme difficulty of analysing, without dazzle or bewilderment, such an unexampled complication of qualities must be admitted as my excuse (2, 782–83).

The failure is, of course, not Byron's but Moore's. Some of the complication of which Moore complains was of his own making. As semiofficial biographer and accessory to the Memoir-burning, he felt he had to bind himself to a principle of wholesale inclusiveness. In order to get materials or to be able to use documents already in his possession, he accepted necessary suppression. Both decisions led him to adopt the inchoate letters-and-journals design. Moore was correct in judging the ruling passion too simpleminded for a complex subject, but he made his subject even more difficult by attempting to squeeze him into a stereotype.

Further complication grew out of Moore's misplaced sense of his own objectivity. He judged himself as biographer "uninfluenced by the peculiar bias supposed to belong to that task" (1, 648). In yet another assertion of the difficulty of his task, he attacked subjective bias as the chief failure of biographical art. "With such abundance and variety of materials . . . it may easily be conceived how two professed delineators of his character, the one over partial and the other malicious, might,—the former, by selecting only the fairer, and the latter only the darker features,—produce two portraits of Lord Byron, as much differing from each other as they would both be, on the whole, unlike the original" (2, 792). In compressing the human Byron to fit the mold of his theory of genius, Moore distorted objectivity as surely as any bias would have. Byron was not Moore's genius thriving on pain any more than he was John Watkins' corrupter of England, or Dallas' petty dilettante.

Moore's final apology is perhaps the most pitifully self-deluding, for here his egotism as guardian of the last word comes to the fore.

> The arduous task of being the biographer of Byron is one, at least, on which I have not obtruded myself: the wish of my friend that I should undertake that office having been more than once expressed, at a time when none but a boding imagination like his could have foreseen much chance of the sad honour devolving to me. If in some instances I have consulted rather the spirit than the exact letter of his injunctions, it was with the view solely of doing him more justice than he would have done himself; there being no hands in which his character could have been less safe than his own, nor any greater wrong offered to his memory than the substitution of what he affected to be for what he was (2, 807).

The failure of Moore's myth of anguished genius lies in the obligation of the genius always to be true to his highest ideal (a requirement as stringent as any Evangelical ideal of perfect virtue, although the terms are different): subsequent disaffection with illusory values or imaginative ideals is a descent from the high plane on which genius lives and breathes at its best.

Moore took the Byron myth almost more seriously than Byron himself. Even Byron allowed for the anti-Romantic. His best poem was *Don Juan,* an experiment in satire and destruction of his own pose of self-concentration, and of that of his heroes—themselves extensions of the myth of what Byron "affected to be." Moore did Byron less justice than he had done himself simply by insisting upon one Byron and denying the other. The full portrait had to wait for the twentieth century's binocular vision to take in both myth and man without denying the one or the other, to see that both were important, both real, both the essential Byron.

CHAPTER SEVEN

LOCKHART'S SCOTT

*The perhaps dismalest thing for me (if I were
to think of myself at all in the matter) is that
very likely, when all his letters are thrown open
to an unscrupulous after age, my manipulation may
be thrown overboard entirely.*

—JOHN GIBSON LOCKHART[1]

John Gibson Lockhart, a familial intimate with a major figure
of nineteenth-century literature, might well have been the
envy of many aspiring biographers. His enviable intimacy,
though, put him on the brink of all the great pitfalls of nineteenth-century biography. Worse even than having been ap-
pointed by the family (as he had been), he had become a member
of the family. Contemporary journalists had good reason to
think he would succumb to the massed forces of eulogy, dignity,
and example. With access to virtually all of Scott's surviving
memorabilia, he might well have been expected to produce yet
another pious and ponderous work, pinpointing chronology,
excising indiscretions, and hacking away at the rough edges
of personality in order to construct a suitable monument to
the deceased in four volumes quarto.

Ultimately he produced seven volumes octavo, but it was
not the expected monument. He refused advice and denied, one
by one, most of the contemporary doctrines of biography. To
create an example, he felt it was only necessary to describe the
man as he knew him, the genius as his intimates remembered
him.

1. Lockhart to Cadell, 20 June 1836: Scott, *Letters*, ed. Herbert Grierson
(1932), *I* [xxvii].

My sole object is to do him justice, or rather, to let him do himself justice, by so contriving it that he shall be, as far as possible, from first to last his own biographer. . . . A stern sense of duty—that kind of sense of it which is combined with the feeling of his actual presence in a serene state of elevation above all petty terrestrial and temporary views— will induce me to touch the few darker points in his life and character as freely as the others which were so predominant; and my chief anxiety on the appearance of the book will be, not to hear what is said by the world, but what is thought by you and the few others who can really compare the representation of the whole with the facts of the case.[2]

In his insistence that Scott speak in his own voice, Lockhart seems to surrender to contemporary fashion, but "by so contriving" is a much more important phrase than it appears to be here. It is the key to his composition.

Lockhart had no sympathy for the contemporary tendency to make the life exemplary no matter what the man had been. He wrote to Benjamin Robert Haydon, just after *Scott* was published:

I trusted to the substantial greatness and goodness of the character, and thought I should only make it more effective in portraiture by keeping in the few specks. I despise with my heels the whole trickery of erecting an alabaster image, and calling that a *Man*. Probably I shall be very severely handled for daring, in the seventh volume, to indicate the decay of his intellectual vigour. But I did this very deliber-

2. Letter to Will Laidlaw, 19 Jan. 1837, quoted in Marion Lochhead, *John Gibson Lockhart* (1954), pp. 208–09. Lochhead had access to a number of unpublished letters, but did not choose to cite specific dates, or, quite often, addressees. The source cited for the chapter in which this letter appears is Abbotsford MSS 1554–55 (1837–40), in the National Library of Scotland. Francis R. Hart dates the letter in "Proofreading Lockhart's Scott: Dynamics of Biographical Reticence," *Studies in Bibliography, 14* (1961), 10–11.

ately, on purpose to show that all the good points of his moral being, and all the predominant trains of fancy and feeling, survived the wreck.[3]

If he but rendered the man complete, the example, he felt, must follow. When it came to the question of dignity, Lockhart's attitude was more complex. As shown in the quotation above, doctrinal dignity having to do with the "honour and glory of the dead" did not press closely upon his conscience. He did, though, formulate some specific biographical standards on the basic question of dignity. McCrone's threatened publication of a *Life of Sir Walter Scott*[4] (before Lockhart finished his life) brought forth a stream of abuse which revealed some clear principles in the matter of dignity similar to Wordsworth's *Letter* and with strikingly similar phrases: "I well knew that altho' you always loved and respected Sir W. you could not write so many pages about him without saying things that would give pain to his children. . . . I felt that you had permitted yourself to put before the public a statement which would cause misery to my wife and her sister."[5] Again, in the text of the *Life of Scott* itself, Lockhart alluded to his respect for the sensitivity of family feelings.

I never thought it lawful to keep a journal of what passes in private society, so that no one need expect from the sequel of this narrative any detailed record of Scott's familiar talk. What fragments of it have happened to adhere to a tolerably retentive memory, and may be put into black and white without wounding any feeling which my friend, were he alive, would have wished to spare, I shall introduce as the occasion

3. Letter dated 11 Feb. 1838, quoted in Andrew Lang, *The Life and Letters of John Gibson Lockhart* (1898), 2, 182.

4. Publication not traced; not found in J. C. Corson, *A Bibliography of Scott* (1943), pp. 40–45.

5. Lockhart to McCrone, quoted in Lochhead, p. 169, no date given; Abbotsford MSS 1552–53 (1832–36) in the National Library of Scotland.

suggests or serves; but I disclaim on the threshold any thing more than this.[6]

It need hardly be added that dignified respect for the sensitivity of the living did not extend far beyond the Scott family circle. The doings of the Brothers Ballantyne (notably John Ballantyne's "pretty Armidas" and his " 'sweet singer of Israel,' " *4,* 168,174) were subject to the most glaring light of investigation.[7]

This sense of dignity, although it did not match Wordsworth's in doctrinaire tone or severity, was important enough to Lockhart for him to formulate a specific rule of distance for each of the several kinds of personal documents used in the *Life of Scott.* Personal materials offered great insight, but the biographer's discretion had to act as interpreter between the subject and the reader. Lockhart refused at the outset to record conversations.

> I . . . wish to register a protest once for all against the general fidelity of several literary gentlemen who have kindly forwarded to me private lucubrations of theirs, designed to *Boswellize* Scott, and which they may probably publish hereafter. To report conversations fairly, it is a necessary prerequisite that we should be completely familiar with all the interlocutors, and understand thoroughly all their mi-

6. *Memoirs of the Life of Sir Walter Scott, Bart.* (7 vols. 1837-38), *4,* 150–51. Subsequent references to this work are given within parentheses in the text.

7. These allusions only added fuel to the fire kindled by Lockhart's treatment of Scott's business dealings. James Ballantyne's trustees protested in *A Refutation of the Mistatements and Calumnies Contained in Mr. Lockhart's Life of Scott respecting the Messrs Ballantyne* (1838). Lockhart answered with *The Ballantyne-humbug Handled, in a Letter to Sir Adam Ferguson* (Edinburgh, 1839). The trustees' *Reply to Mr Lockhart's Pamphlet* followed the same year. The complex issue of ultimate responsibility for the financial collapse has not yet been resolved (see Grierson's introduction, *Letters,* 1932, *1,* xxxiii–xlix; James Glen's note on "Scott's Financial Transactions," ibid., *1* [lxxx]–xcv; and Grierson, *Sir Walter Scott, Bart.,* 1938, passim).

nutest relations, and points of common knowledge, and common feeling, with each other. He who does not, must be perpetually in danger of misinterpreting sportive allusion into serious statement; and the man who was only recalling, by some jocular phrase or half-phrase, to an old companion, some trivial reminiscence of their boyhood or youth, may be represented as expressing, upon some person or incident casually tabled, an opinion which he had never framed, or if he had, would never have given words to in any mixed assemblage—not even among what the world calls *friends* at his own board. . . . For this one reason, to say nothing of many others, I consider no man justified in journalizing what he sees and hears in a domestic circle where he is not thoroughly at home; and I think there are still higher and better reasons why he should not do so where he is (*4*, 151).

Lockhart had pronounced the *Life of Johnson* to be "about the richest dictionary of wit and wisdom any language can boast,"[8] but he did not sanction Boswell's methods. In the next few pages he even goes out of his way to get in digs at Boswell.[9] Although he avoided comments upon the biographer's personal failings in his review of Croker's edition, Lockhart evidently sympathized in general with the contemporary opinion that Boswell's innovation was one that biography might well have been spared.

Although Lockhart distrusted letters, he did not accept Wordsworth's sentiments on epistolary candor generally. He depends most heavily upon Scott's letters for his "own voice": "I return to the copious and candid correspondence from which it has been throughout my object to extract and combine the scattered fragments of an *autobiography*" (*5*, 178). This public faith in Scott's· self-objectivity, however, was subject to some private qualification. "In the latter volumes I shall have more

8. Review of Croker's edition of Boswell, *Quarterly Review*, *46* (1831), 46.

9. "Sir Alexander Boswell of Auchinleck, . . . had all his father *Bozzy's* cleverness, good humour, and joviality, without one touch of his meaner qualities" (*4*, 159); "Dr. Johnson and his bearleader" (*4*, 160).

of my own and your recollections to draw on and (having already sufficiently exhibited his epistolary vein) may draw more moderately on that source of at least doubtful information as to the real feelings of one who *in his later days* must have felt that whatever he wrote would one day perhaps be printed."[1] Such misgivings demonstrate that he had given some thought to dignity before deciding what weight he could give letters. Dignity seems to have been most important to the intermediary decisions which shaped his biographical method for the *Life of Scott*—not so much as a final arbiter of what ought or ought not be told.

Lockhart took up Scott's journal with only slightly less trepidation than he felt concerning conversation.

> The reader cannot expect that any chapter in a Diary of this sort should be printed *in extenso* within a few years of the writer's death. The editor has, for reasons which need not be explained, found it necessary to omit some passages altogether—to abridge others—and very frequently to substitute asterisks or arbitrary initials for names. But wherever omissions or alterations have been made, these were dictated by regard for the feelings of living persons; and, if any passages which have been retained should prove offensive to such feelings, there is no apology to be offered, but that the editor found they could not be struck out, without losing some statement of fact, opinion, or sentiment, which it seemed impossible to sacrifice without injustice to Sir Walter Scott's character and history (*6, 123*).

That he feels the reader will immediately recognize and sympathize with his general temerity concerning a journal is a measure of the force of dignity in 1837. But the rest of the statement places this respect for dignity in a clearly defined hierarchy of biographical principles. Dignity should be respected: the biographer should not descend to personal inti-

---

1. Letter to Cadell, 20 June 1836, quoted in Grierson's introduction to *Letters* (1932), *1* [xxvii].

macies, *except* where they are essential to his subject's "character and history." This leaves room to the biographer, of course, for a breadth of discretionary suppression, and a breadth of interpretation as to what is "essential" and what is not. But he establishes, more firmly than do most contemporary biographers, his primary allegiance: not to the immortal souls of his readers, not to the feelings of the subject's family and friends, not to the pains of the living, but to the truth of his image of the subject.

Dignity was important to Lockhart but it was subservient to his guiding principle, his image of Scott. He maintains a clear supremacy of artistic aims over ethical reservations which should not be forgotten in judging some of his more questionable "manipulations."

The relationship between Lockhart's biographical method and Boswell's has been thoroughly discussed by Francis R. Hart,[2] so there is no need to dwell upon it at any length here. In general, the similarities between Lockhart and Boswell are perhaps less important than the dissimilarities. Lockhart connects his subject's first-person documents with his own chronological narrative, as does Boswell. He quotes other published accounts of events, or the testimony of outside witnesses, perhaps more willingly than Boswell, but is just as quick to point out that he is the only bearer of the truth when he finds other narrators in error. Thomas Moore and Lord Byron are put down at once in a matter of dating,[3] and a few pages later Lockhart discounts false reports of Scott's dinner with George IV, gathering about him all the authority of his position as official chronicler, and some of the tone of the outraged Boswell: "This story has been circulated in a very perverted shape. I now give it on

2. "Boswell and the Romantics," *ELH*, 27 (1960), 44.

3. "Lord Byron accompanied [Joanna Baillie] . . . and Mr and Mrs Scott to [Miss Baillie's tragedy] . . . and . . . the vase with the Attic bones appears to have been sent to Scott very soon after his arrival in London, not, as Mr Moore had gathered from the hasty diction of his 'Reminiscences,' at some 'subsequent period of their acquaintance.' This is sufficiently proved by the following note" (3, 339).

the authority of my venerated friend [William Adam], who was—unlike, perhaps, some others of the company at that hour —able to hear accurately, and content to *see single*" (*3, 343*).

Lockhart's refusal "to *Boswellize* Scott" presents a disagreement in biographical principles far more profound than simple distaste for "journalizing" conversation. Boswell conceived his book in dramatic terms. This was perhaps necessitated by his wealth of conversational material, but it seems also to have been his most characteristic approach to experience. His many roles ("Be *retinu*"), his affection for costuming (Corsica Boswell), his sense of dramatic timing (interruptions in his amour with Louisa) in the journals indicate that the dramatic mode was for him less a literary method than an inherent pattern of perception. Johnson's talk organized scenes, in which Boswell appeared dramatically together with the rest of the participants. Boswell acting his role in the *Life* differs from Boswell the biographer. The dramatic Boswell introduces conversational topics and makes ridiculous observations in order to draw out the great man. He is content to appear a fool to the other actors in his drama, and often to his readers, for the sake of the profits which accrue for his journal, and ultimately for his *Life*. Boswell creates a dramatic persona for the sake of his book.

Lockhart's milieu was not dramatic, so there is no reason to expect the *Life of Scott* to take on dramatic structure. He seldom appears in his book, and the self-depiction is so slight and shadowy that he never really emerges as a character, much less as a dramatic persona. He appeals to his relationship with Scott only enough to establish his authority as an authority on the novelist. Lockhart is innocent of the allusions Boswell makes to "my great friend"; even more surprising, he almost never refers to Scott as "my father-in-law." Lockhart gives the greater *impression* of objectivity.

Whenever he makes his infrequent appearances, however, his presence produces an intensity of narrative. Such scenes stand out as three-dimensional islands surrounded by what appears to be, at first reading, two-dimensional objectivity. His opinions, observations, participation, take on added power because of the reserve with which he introduces them. These islands of participation seem to attract the rest of the book toward themselves: to animate and organize the chronological narrative, the letters, the journal, and descriptions by other observers.

These are the passages which immediately come to mind when looking back on the *Life of Scott:* the rather long digression on Scott's den and his dinner parties that follows Lockhart's description of his first meeting with him (*4*, 145 ff.); Lockhart's first visit to Abbotsford (*4*, 185–203); the description of Constable in the heat of enthusiasm for his *Miscellany* (*6*, 28–32). The sense of doom with which Lockhart endows his description of Scott's financial folly before the collapse certainly partakes of this first-person immediacy (*5*, 148–49). Of course, the two scenes attendant upon the actual collapse[4] (which Herbert Grierson so brilliantly proves to be at best questionable, at worst sheer invention)[5] derive vitality from Lockhart's acknowledged presence. The whole chronicle of Scott's financial difficulties owes its pathos and its inexorable, almost tragic movement to these scenes. There are other moments at which Lockhart steps briefly into the narrative and delivers himself of opinions: his apostrophe on the death of Mrs. Lockhart introduced in the fifth volume (125); and his almost inexplicable appearance to comment upon Scott's introduction of gaslight at Abbotsford (*5*, 267–68).

The difference between Boswell's and Lockhart's active presence is but a part of a greater difference in approach. Where Boswell conceives the movement of his *Life* as drama—in dialogue, dramatic incident, and revelation of characters through speech—Lockhart's approach is essentially novelistic.

---

4. Lockhart's warning to Scott of impending disaster and Scott's dramatic journey to Polton (*6*, 104 ff.); and Lockhart's interview with Constable (*6*, 174 ff.).

5. "Lang, Lockhart, and Biography," in *Essays and Addresses* (1940), pp. 144–50. For another interpretation of Lockhart's "dramatization," see Francis R. Hart, ".Proofreading Lockhart's Scott," *Studies in Bibliography*, *14* (1961), 13–16.

Lockhart's first visit to Abbotsford is perhaps the best demonstration of the biographer's novelistic sense.

It was near the dinner-hour before we reached the house, and presently I saw assembled a larger company than I should have fancied to be at all compatible with the existing accommodations of the place; but it turned out that Captain Ferguson, and the friends whom I have not as yet mentioned, were to find quarters elsewhere for the night. His younger brother, Captain John Ferguson of the Royal Navy (a favourite lieutenant of Lord Nelson's), had come over from Huntly Burn; there were present also, Mr Scott of Gala, whose residence is within an easy distance; Sir Henry Hay MacDougal of Mackerstone, an old baronet with gay, lively, and highly polished manners, related in the same degree to both Gala and the Sheriff; Sir Alexander Don, the member for Roxburghshire, whose elegant social qualities have been alluded to in the preceding chapter; and Dr Scott of Darnlee, a modest and intelligent gentleman who having realized a fortune in the East India Company's medical service, had settled within two or three miles of Abbotsford, and though no longer practising his profession, had kindly employed all the resources of his skill in the endeavour to counteract his neighbour's recent liability to attacks of cramp (*4*, 187–88).[6]

The characters are introduced. To compare this brief passage with the great minor characterizations of fiction would be to ridicule it. It is not and does not strive to be their equal, but it is of their kind. Each member of the party is identified with a brief phrase. The reader might wish to know more about some; some, we are reminded, have already been introduced. It is the kind of introduction Jane Austen might permit herself for characters who were not going to concern her too much, before she really got down to the business at hand. It is just

6. The impression of novelistic approach which *Scott* gives might justify further study of the relationship between the biography and Lockhart's early novels, *Valerius: A Roman story, Adam Blair, Reginald Dalton,* and *Matthew Wald.*

enough to give the comfort of real surroundings, and the feeling of verisimilitude, without distracting the reader from the real interest.

—Our host and one or two others appeared, as was in those days a common fashion with country gentlemen, in the lieutenancy uniform of their county. How fourteen or fifteen people contrived to be seated in the then dining-room of Abbotsford I know not—for it seemed quite full enough when it contained only eight or ten; but so it was—nor, as Sir Harry Macdougal's fat valet, warned by former experience, did not join the train of attendants, was there any perceptible difficulty in the detail of the arrangements. Every thing about the dinner was, as the phrase runs, in excellent style; and in particular, the *potage à la Meg Merrilees,* announced as an attempt to imitate a device of the Duke of Buccleuch's celebrated cook—by name Monsieur Florence— seemed, to those at least who were better acquainted with the Kaim of Derncleuch than with the *cuisine* of Bowhill, a very laudable specimen of the art (*4,* 188–89).

A feeling of the crowded dining room suggested by a familiar allusion to a domestic; the comfortable familiarity of a dinner party with none of the conversation, but again, only suggestion.

The champagne circulated nimbly—and I never was present at a gayer dinner. It had advanced a little beyond the soup when it received an accompaniment which would not, perhaps, have improved the satisfaction of Southern guests, had any such been present. A tall and stalwart bagpiper, in complete Highland costume, appeared pacing to and fro on the green before the house, and the window being open, it seemed as if he might as well have been straining his lungs within the parlour. At a pause of his strenuous performance, Scott took occasion to explain that *John of Skye* was a recent acquisition to the rising hamlet of Abbotstown; that the man was a capital hedger and ditcher, and only figured with the pipe and philabeg on high occasions in the after-part of the day; "but indeed," he added, laughing, "I fear John will soon be discovering that the hook and mattock are unfavourable to his chanter hand." When the cloth was drawn, and the never-failing salver of *quaighs* introduced, John of Skye, upon some well-known signal, entered the room, but *en militaire,* without removing his bonnet, and taking his station behind the landlord, received from his hand the largest of the Celtic bickers brimful of Glenlivet. The man saluted the company in his own dialect, tipped off the contents (probably a quarter of an English pint of raw aquavitae) at a gulp, wheeled about as solemnly as if the whole ceremony had been a movement on parade, and forthwith recommenced his pibrochs and gatherings, which continued until long after the ladies had left the table, and the autumnal moon was streaming in upon us so brightly as to dim the candles *(4,* 189–90).

One striking difference in the novelistic approach is the sense it gives of surroundings. Boswell dresses his scenes for the most part with no more than the characters and a few hand properties (a punch bowl, a hat, a few books, a pot of tea), and rightly so. Anything more would be surplus for his kind of narrative. A stronger and more detailed background is necessary for Lockhart, or the whole structure of these scenes would collapse. The background is the novelist's setting rather than the dramatist's stage directions.

I had never before seen Scott in such buoyant spirits as he showed this evening—and I never saw him in higher afterwards; and no wonder, for this was the first time that he, Lord Melville, and Adam Ferguson, daily companions at the High-school of Edinburgh, and partners in many joyous scenes of the early volunteer period, had met since the commencement of what I may call the serious part of any of their lives. The great poet and novelist was receiving them under his own roof, when his fame was at its *acmé,* and his fortune seemed culminating to about a corresponding height—and the generous exuberance of his hilarity might have overflowed without moving the spleen of a Cynic. Old stories of *the Yards* and *the Crosscauseway* were relieved by sketches of real warfare, such as none but Ferguson (or Charles Matthews, had he been a soldier) could ever have given; and they toasted the memory of *Greenbreeks* and the health of *the Beau* with equal devotion.

When we rose from table, Scott proposed that we should all ascend his western turret, to enjoy a moonlight view of the valley. The younger part of his company were too happy to do so: some of the seniors, who had tried the thing before, found pretexts for hanging back. The stairs were dark, narrow, and steep; but the Sheriff piloted the way, and at length there were as many on the top as it could well afford footing for. Nothing could be more lovely than the panorama; all the harsher and more naked features being lost in the delicious moonlight; the Tweed and the Gala winding and sparkling beneath our feet; and the distant ruins of Melrose appearing, as if carved of alabaster, under the black mass of the Eildons. The poet, leaning on his battlement, seemed to hang over the beautiful vision as if he had never seen it before. "If I live," he exclaimed, "I will build me a higher tower, with a more spacious platform, and a staircase better fitted for an old fellow's scrambling." The piper was heard retuning his instrument below, and he called to him for *Lochaber no more.* John of Skye obeyed, and as the music rose, softened by the distance, Scott repeated in a low key the melancholy words of the song of exile (*4,* 190–91).

The scope of dramatic scene was too narrow and its setting too sparsely dressed for Lockhart and, perhaps, for Scott. The novel's potential for mood, color, and suggestion better fitted his talents as biographer, and better fitted the nature of his subject and his imaginative vision of this nature. By the suggestion that Scott is here at the *"acmé"* of fame and that "his fortune seemed culminating to about a corresponding height" Lockhart projects the tragedy to come. After this suggestion, the western turret takes on a symbolic quality which is inescapable. It is Scott's construction of a dream—a dream involved with Scott the laird and Scott the Scotsman, but inevitably dependent upon Scott the writing machine.

The *Life of Scott* has few such scenes, but Boswell's *Life* is not all conversations either. Lockhart's "islands of participation" control the book and determine its course, even as Boswell's scenes built around Johnson's talk organize his book. By the reserve with which Lockhart introduces himself, he is able to have it both ways: to be both a participant and an objective, removed observer. By avoiding an obtrusive persona, Lockhart combats the charge of partisanship and eulogy inevitably leveled at him. He does not develop himself as a character in his chronicle, and so enforces the appearance of objectivity. At the same time, we never forget he is Scott's son-in-law. He scatters his name through the narrative with an almost random familiarity, and his presence is felt just enough to confirm his authority as the bearer of the truth. Boswell announced his objectivity and inserted himself as an integral dramatic participant in his book. Lockhart dissociates himself from the proceedings in order to establish his objectivity tacitly, but his presence intensifies the narrative, often unexpectedly, so that the reader cannot forget his authority.

A literary device which is as characteristic of Lockhart as his novelistic approach is the impression he conveys of a writer engaged, even while he writes, in the process of discovering the truth. He announces in his conclusion to the *Life* that he hesitates, even here, to make observations of his own, because it has been his intention from the beginning to let the book take its own shape, to let Scott's "sayings and doings," and his letters and diaries (rather than the biographer's comment) reveal his character, "conscious that I have wilfully withheld nothing that might assist the mature reader to arrive at just conclusions, I am by no means desirous of drawing out a detailed statement of my own" (7, 398).

When Lockhart, earlier, begins his narration of Scott's financial collapse, he suggests that he comes to these revelations as innocent as the reader. "I had . . . no notion, until all his correspondence lay before me, of the extent to which he had permitted himself thus early to build on the chances of life, health, and continued popularity (5, 149)." He proceeds to narrate the details of catastrophe with the tone of the shocked discoverer: every new clue he finds among the letters and accounts seems a revelation, as he reflects upon the emotions and opinions that he had experienced at the time. He tells the reader he is confused by certain aspects of the whole chain of events: "It is the extent to which the confusion had gone that constitutes the great puzzle (6, 115)." Throughout the book, the reader is conscious that he is accompanying Lockhart on a mission of discovery.

In no other biography, perhaps, does the reader feel so strongly that he is witnessing, or rather, experiencing with the biographer, the formation of his final impressions on the subject—really a new synthesis of his personal impressions in the light of all the documentary evidence. There are certain assumptions about Scott's character which are, for Lockhart, preconceptions (that is, formed before he began composition): Scott as the almost feudal paterfamilias with his family and tenants, Scott the antiquarian, Scott the Scotsman, Scott the writing machine, and Scott the genius of literature and of human nature. But these preconceptions, taken as given quantities very near the outset of the book, are developed with the financial collapse of 1826 in mind. Upon reaching this point of crisis, Lockhart indicates the necessity for readjustment of these given characteristics. He invites the reader to share with him the formation of a new synthesis—taking each of the former characteristics, tracing its progress through the disaster, and observing how it emerges after the collapse.

Scott depended upon his prolific literary genius to provide for the construction and continuation of his antiquarian ideal —his dream of the reconstruction of the surroundings, the atmosphere, the family and estate relationships of the past. With his literary fame and his efforts to foster appreciation of national history came a certain elevation of social and financial fortunes which made possible the realization of that dream. The development of parts of this concept and their formation into an ideal, the construction of a way of life—a dream almost realized—is sharply broken by the collapse of 1826. The remainder of the biography, and the remainder of Scott's life, are concerned with the reexamination of the foundations of that dream and an attempt to salvage something from the wreckage of the financial fortune that made it possible.

Whether Lockhart already knew the details of the transactions, of which he now pretends discovery, is immaterial. By the interpolation of the biographer's discovery and amazement, which give the impression of synchronous formulation and composition—more particularly, by the realization of the necessity for a new synthesis at the moment of collapse—Lockhart involves his readers in Scott's fortunes.

This suggestion of the biographer in process is so slight in proportion to the work as a whole that perhaps it does not justify so much critical attention. However slight, though, it is an almost perfect example of Stanfield's "biographical spirit"[7] —a spirit which goes beyond the biographer's interest in his subject to convey his enthusiasm, his involvement in his subject's fortunes, ultimately transmitted by the biography and reproduced in the reader. As an attempt to reproduce the process of artistic decision and creative synthesis, it follows a pattern made familiar in Wordsworth's *The Prelude*. Even as Wordsworth's poem intends to impress the reader with the moment and the emotions of creation, so Lockhart's narrative engages us in a creative moment of biographical synthesis. Perhaps it is design or device, perhaps accident; perhaps he really is discovering and resynthesizing as he writes. But, in any event, his account of Scott's last years, a personal odyssey which comes close to tragedy, would not engage us as it does without the sense of the biographer in process.

Carlyle characterized the *Life of Scott* as a mere compilation, useful in its kind, but not bearing the mark of the artist's composing touch.[8] He was certainly too much prejudiced by the length of Lockhart's work, but it is understandable that

7. See above, Chapter Four, pp. 69–70.
8. See above, p. 80.

he would not acknowledge the book as a masterwork. The very contemporaneity of publication which enforced the doctrine of dignity and dictated so many bad biographies, concealed Lockhart's literary artistry in the *Life of Scott*. Since it was impossible to reveal all the material from which Lockhart drew his portrait, his "composition" remained hidden. We are in a much better position to perceive the artistic elements at work in Lockhart's book today than were his contemporaries, since the mass of materials from which he drew his *Scott* is available for examination.

Denying himself Boswell's ever present dramatic persona and his conversational dramas, denying himself the obvious touch of the biographer's exhortation and moralizing which Carlyle regarded as essential to "composition,"[9] Lockhart turned to a mode of composition which he felt was the only one left to him: arrangement, silent ellipsis of documents, and imaginative dramatization. Unable or unwilling to be an actor because he prized so highly the quality (or at least the appearance) of objectivity, Lockhart became instead a powerful stage manager. His subject was to speak in his own voice, but Lockhart retained the right to clap his hand over Scott's mouth when he pleased, to arrange statements in an order which suited his plan, sentiments in a style which agreed with his guiding principle: his image of Scott.

Depending upon Scott's epistolary correspondence for the bulk of his narrative, he felt it his privilege as biographer to splice letters together with little regard for correspondent or date, in much the same manner as the modern recording engineer can splice recording tape, and with results which appear similarly close to misrepresentation. Davidson Cook details one example of Lockhart's method of aggregation, in which parts of a letter dated 10 April [1827] are inserted in the text of a letter of 26 April.[1] Both letters were addressed to Lockhart,

9. For Carlyle's distinction between "compilation" and "composition," see above, p. 80.

1. "Lockhart's Treatment of Scott's Letters," *Nineteenth Century, 102* (1927), 391–96; *Letters* (1932), *10*, 182–85, 196–98. For Lockhart's version, see *Scott, 7*, 30–31.

and ellipsis was indicated at the beginning (where a sentence of the first letter was omitted) and again in the middle (indicating an omission in the second letter). A few lines of verse not found in either letter are also inserted. That both were letters to Lockhart hardly acquits him of deliberate misrepresentation. Other examples of this sort of editorial aggregation can be found throughout the *Life of Scott*.[2]

He seems to have regarded documents as his raw materials, even as he had considered reviewers' manuscripts submitted to him for the *Quarterly* to be first drafts, subject to whatever changes he felt necessary.[3] As biographer, he edited with an eye to the text's conformity to his image of Scott: combining a page here and there of different letters, changing Scott's own words where he felt they lent the wrong impression, cutting whatever passages seemed trivial, irrelevant, or out of keeping with his view of Scott at the time.

Such "manipulation," as Grierson terms it (using Lockhart's own word) occurred at almost every point in the book. It is not possible to find an example representative of all of Lockhart's principles of selection, but a letter showing two stages of selection (original transcription and proof revision) reflects, perhaps as well as any single example could, something of the progress of selective "manipulation." Passages bracketed were omitted from the *Life;* italicized words are Lockhart's own additions.

TO MR JOHN BALLANTYNE

Abbotsford 16 Augt. 1813

Dear John,— [I received all your letters & hope the business with Mr[4] Innes is settled if not I shall send a Drat to Mr[4] Fair.

2. Grierson's notes to the *Letters* (1932) detail many of these.

3. One of the letters telescoped, cited above (26 April 1827), contains Scott's authorization to Lockhart to edit freely one of his reviews: "You know you can 'dumple the inclosed as you list' " (*Letters*, 1932, *10*, 198). Francis R. Hart in "Proofreading Lockhart's Scott" defends Lockhart's editorial attitude to documents.

4. Grierson supplies the "r" of "Mr" in square brackets, here omitted to avoid confusion.

This will greatly hurt my means of getting supplies in the country but the resolution I have now taken renders that of less consequence.] I am quite satisfied it is impossible for Jo: B. & Co/ to continue business longer than is absolutely necessary for the sale of stock & extrication of their affairs. The fatal injury which their credit has sustained as well as your adopting a profession in which I sincerely [trust] *hope* you will be more fortunate renders the closing of the book-selling business inevitable. With regard to the printing it is my intention to retire *from that also* so soon as I can possibly do so with safety to myself and with the regard I shall always entertain for James's interest. Whatever loss I may sustain will be preferable to the life I have lately led when I seem surrounded by a sort of magic circle which neither permits me to remain at home in peace nor to stir abroad with pleasure. [I have therefore resolved that all [the][5] *my* copyrights *shall* be sold and I have to request you will take the necessary [measures][5] *steps* for doing so immediately & to the best advantage: perhaps Longman should have the refusal you may consider this. As Gale is now down & Rees will soon be so you will certainly have it in your power to make a bargain as well as if you were in London, or you may speak to Blackwood & Constable also: though I fear the latter is too deeply dipd to make it possible at this time for him to be a purchaser. Get rid of them however at such dates as will bring in cash for the exigencies of the business without giving me any farther trouble. I should imagine if you proceed cautiously they will fetch long prices. As I hereby give up our bargain of sale the Compy will fall to retire the drats. I granted so far as still outstandy. & to repay me the sums I have advanced for paymt. of the £3700.

If the money thus procured is inadequate to the relief of these affairs] your first exertions [will] *may* probably be [made] on 'that distinguished select and inimitable collection of books made by an amateur of this city retiring from

5. Lockhart's changes in originally transcribing the letter. He eventually decided to omit the whole passage (see below).

business.' I do not have either health or confidence in my own powers sufficient to authorize me to take a long price for a new poem untill these affairs shall have been in some measure digested. This idea has been long running in my head but the late fatalities which have attended this business have quite decided my resolution. [Probably the copy rights may carry some stock with them if well managed.] I will write to James tomorrow being at present annoyd with a severe headache. Yours truly

W. Scott

[I trust I shall be able to get cash for the exigencies after the 24th. I wish to know if the £612 of bills stated in the calendar as at maturity in Septr. are to be brought forwd. in the beginning of the month or how?—][6]

Of these omissions, the first cut and that of the postscript were probably dictated by a desire for brevity. These are business details with little significance in Scott's "fatal connexion with merchandise" (as Lockhart so dramatically puts it, 7, 403). The suggestion that Ballantyne offer the copyrights to Longmans is perhaps cut because of contemporaneity: this was in the character of a trade secret. The rest of the excisions, however, seem to have been made in the interests of "composition." In manuscript (or in an earlier proof) Lockhart attempted to soften somewhat the suggestion of the sale of copyrights. He does not hesitate to alter the wording of his text to accomplish this: substitution of "shall be sold" for "be sold" and "steps" for "measures" are his own innovation, without authority in Scott's text. In reading the proofs, when he had a better sense

6. *Scott, 3,* 73–74; *Letters* (1932), *1,* 437–38. The proof sheets, in the possession of Frederick W. Hilles, are bound in six volumes. For the most part, these correspond to what we know as page proofs, printed on recto only. Volume 4 contains only the first 228 pages of the published volume 4, but all of published 5, designated as "final proofs," printed on recto and verso, and trimmed. The proofs for the remainder of published 4 are wanting. A full discussion of the proofs with detailed description and recovery of deleted passages is given by Francis R. Hart, "Proofreading Lockhart's Scott."

of the context (at least the context of the first three volumes) and a clearer impression of his image of Scott, he decided that the suggestion of sale of the copyrights did not agree with his view of Scott at this time, so he cut all such suggestions in proof.[7] The completed image is not realized all at once. Selection for interest, and cuts to avoid offense to the living are made at the outset, but final "composition" to bring the printed depiction of Scott into line with Lockhart's mental image is going on all the time, up to and including the final proofs. None of the ellipses is indicated in the *Life*.

In the journals, there is less evidence of this sort of last-minute "manipulation." A comparison of Lockhart's excerpts with the 1939 edition of the *Journals* for January 1826 reveals some omission of trivial matters ("Jane Russel[l] drank tea with us"),[8] and of medical entries ("Anne ill of rheumatism: I believe caught cold by vexation and exposing herself to bad weather"),[9] but little which may clearly be called concealment or suppression. A cut which is perhaps motivated by an aim beyond that of brevity and relevance has to do with Constable.

> Edinburgh, January 16.—Came through cold roads to as cold news. Hurst and Robinson have suffered a bill [of £1000] to come back upon Constable, which I suppose infers the ruin of both houses. We will soon see. [Constable, it seems, who was to have set off in the last week of December, dawdled here till in all human probability his going or staying became a matter of mighty little consequence. He could not be there till Monday night, and his resources must have come too late.] Dined with the Skenes. . . .
> January 19.—. . . Letters from Constable and Robinson have arrived. The last persist in saying they will pay all and everybody. They say, moreover, in a postscript, that had Constable

7. In a letter of 24 Aug. 1813 (*3*, 76), Lockhart cuts out "In fact, six months would clear us, even without sale of the old copyrights & stock."

8. *The Journal of Sir Walter Scott, 1825–26, the Text Revised from a Photostat in the National Library of Scotland*, ed. J. G. Tait (1939), p. 82; *Scott*, *6*, 202.

9. *Journal*, p. 82.

been in town ten days sooner, all would have been well. [When I saw him on 24th December, he proposed starting in three days, but dallied, God knows why, in a kind of infatuation, I think, till things had got irretrievably wrong. There would have been no want of support here and his stock under his own management would have made a return immensely greater than it can under any other. Now[1] I fear the loss must be great, as his fall will involve many of the country dealers who traded with him.][2]

Taking into account Lockhart's treatment of Constable elsewhere in the book ("on the brink of insanity," 6, 177), it seems unlikely that Lockhart made these cuts out of a regard for the delicacy of the living. There seem to be two factors involved here: Scott's realization of Constable's culpable neglect in the face of financial disaster (the revelation of which Lockhart perhaps wanted to soften, or at least to delay); and Scott's ever kind and even temper. The tone of the journals at this point is one of quiet resignation in the face of disaster, and the personal note of impatience introduced by the excised passages perhaps destroys, or at least dilutes, that tone. Since Scott's diary narrative precedes Lockhart's parallel narrative, the cut is probably made in the interests of timing.[3] Lockhart's biographical approach does not push his own personality into the foreground, but it is understandable that he might wish to reserve the whole question of Constable's negligence for his own analysis. Though perhaps less justifiable in ethical than in artistic terms, the timing of revelation, assessment, and final analysis is central to Lockhart's narrative vitality, the key to the tempo of his biography. The islands of participation, the "muffled drum" (5, 418) of financial collapse, the measured,

1. Scott underlined "Now"; omitted from this transcription to avoid confusion with Lockhart's additions.

2. *Journal*, pp. 69–70, 71–72; *Scott, 6,* 191, 193.

3. The cuts might also be involved in Lockhart's "dramatization" of his scene with Constable, since it depends upon the timing of Constable's movements only a month later (see below, p. 149; and Herbert Grierson, "Lang, Lockhart, and Biography," in *Essays and Addresses,* 1940, pp. 148–50).

heroic tempo of Scott's final return to Abbotsford, all demonstrate the novelist's timing of incident and revelation. It was an aim in his "composition" second only to the ultimate design of re-creating his mental image of Scott.

As Grierson demonstrates, it seems likely that Lockhart's novelistic sense carried him even farther into questionable biographical practice. Scott's dramatic ride to Polton to discover the true state of his finances is apparently sheer invention; the same seems to be true of Lockhart's interview with Constable.[4] There is at least well-founded suspicion that Lockhart not only invented Scott's final dying words, but that he invented them to order, on a pattern suggested by a letter from one of Scott's female relatives.[5]

Even conventional regard for the truth as an absolute ideal convicts Lockhart of misrepresentation. In telescoping and fragmentizing letters, Lockhart is perhaps too liable to our twentieth-century respect for the strict inviolability of text. As Grierson points out,[6] had he done less (that is, had he indicated no ellipses, identified no correspondents, quoted no dates in the texts of letters), he would have committed no crime against the truth. As it is, though, with some ellipses indicated and others made silently, with letters telescoped and moved out of their true chronological order, we are ready to believe the worst: concealment and suppression. He treated his sources with an abandoned laissez-faire. If the text did not read well in proof, Lockhart corrected it without reference to the original. He seems to have adhered to the principle that it was his book —letters, journal, and all.

The essential element in suppression is concealment. Whether Lockhart's concealment was designed to a particular nonartistic

4. Grierson, pp. 144–50; *Scott, 6,* 104 ff., 174 ff.

5. Grierson, *Sir Walter Scott, Bart. A New Life Supplementary to, and Corrective of, Lockhart's Biography* (1938), pp. 299–300.

6. "Lang, Lockhart, and Biography," in *Essays and Addresses,* pp. 140–41. See also Robert Rait's qualified defense of Lockhart against some of Davidson Cook's more violent charges in "Boswell and Lockhart," in *Essays by Divers Hands,* new series, 12 (1933), 105–27.

end remains a question for further study, but that it was a product of the pressure of contemporaneity seems clear. Lockhart did not destroy documents. In fact he was quite aware that his concealments, excisions, and perhaps even his dramatizations would eventually be discovered. The epigraph to this chapter contains a clear statement to that effect.

He was motivated by a higher ideal, too. He was the first at the letters and journals, and could use any of them in any manner he chose to support, document, and develop his conception of Sir Walter Scott. He manipulated and called it manipulation, because he knew others would come after him to expose the whole correspondence, the whole journal, the whole story. Now, for a moment, the world had to wait while he formed his image of Scott, while he connected his name irrevocably with the poet's. Using the materials he felt appropriate at the time, composing them in accordance with his conception of the whole man as he had known him and as he now saw him through his intimate papers, shaping his narrative with the artistic sense of a novelist, Lockhart devoted all his powers and his full attention to the realization on paper of an artistic ideal: his image of Scott. It was an image later writers and editors could amend, correct, and annotate, but they could never change it.

The biographer gives form and continuity to the disjointed, seemingly irrelevant confusions of life as it is lived. The biographer looks on the man, examines his documents, and connects threads into a coherent pattern. The whole story can never be told coherently, because the whole story—without the touch of a biographer's selectivity, without organization—is only the confusion of all a man's days. Selection and form are his art. In order to select, he must omit; to give form, some things must be emphasized, others glossed over.

It must be admitted, however, that Lockhart went beyond the latitude of selectivity normally accorded the biographer. His devotion to truth is not relatively less than Boswell's, but of a different kind. Boswell feels free to select the details which concur with his imaginative vision of Johnson, and to give them emphasis by interpretation and arrangement, to support the general character as he sees it. He sees in Edmund Hector's notes (on Johnson as a schoolboy) an element of superiority. He shapes this in gradual revisions until it emerges in the final draft as intellectual superiority.[7] He will play down some of the manifestations of Johnson's dark side, but he will never omit mention of them. Boswell has a keen sense of dramatic timing. He molds his conversations with this tempo in mind, but he does not invent incidents. In one of the most memorable scenes in the *Life of Johnson,* Goldsmith's quarrel with Johnson, Goldsmith hurls down his hat and makes a dramatic departure. In the finished draft this comes as a highly dramatic moment; in the notes for the journal, the action is mentioned in general terms—"he once threw hat w! vengeance on floor"—with no indication of its place in the sequence of the scene.[8] Boswell does not misrepresent, or alter fact to dramatize. A good case can be made, indeed, that he did not add to (or "dramatize") his journal at all, but used it as a mnemonic outline, filling in the gaps of journal with his memory of the incident that the journal had triggered. It is clear (if Grierson's assertions on Lockhart's dramatizations are true) that Lockhart's sense of the biographer's freedom is different in kind.

What then of truth for its own sake? The seeker after truth must deplore such manipulations, but he must then forgive them and admit that they are minor even after he has discovered the hoax. I am far from insisting that truth need not and on the whole ought not be considered a prime virtue of the biographer. But since the whole truth cannot be rendered, since what is valued in biography is as much the biographer's skill in extracting meaning and molding form from the random disorder of a life as it is the subject's innate qualities, the

7. *Life of Johnson,* ed. Hill-Powell (1934), *1,* 47–48; manuscript of the *Life* (with the Boswell Papers, Yale University Library), pp. 11–13; manuscript "Notes" by Hector, enclosed in a letter to Boswell 1 Feb. 1785 (also in Boswell Papers).

8. *Life of Johnson* (1934), 2, 249–56; Boswell's notes for journal, 7 May 1773; manuscript of *Life,* p. 411.

reader must make allowance in his criticism for biographer's license. Lockhart's *Scott* is a great work of art. In the truth of the form, in Lockhart's truth in rendering his mental image of Scott, there is more than enough to compensate for contemporaneous suppression and for literal truth compromised in lies, inventions, and manipulations.

Southey and Lockhart both wrote biographies which have been called masterpieces by that "unscrupulous after age," but the difference between their books only serves to demonstrate once again that there are as few infallible rules, as few tricks of the trade, to great biography as there are infallible knacks to any other art. Southey wrote his biography with no more than the most distant acquaintance with Nelson; Lockhart wrote from an intimate familiarity of fourteen years. Southey's principle of selection was based upon the exclusion of all facts and incidents which seemed to him to be irrelevant; he worked with an established, published compilation of materials and attempted to extract from it the essential elements of his subject's deeds, personality, and character. Lockhart's selection had, of necessity, an opposite direction; with the family's monopoly of Scott documents, he attempted, by the inclusion of everything relevant, to relate the parts, diverse incidents, and irregularities to the whole of his memory and his imaginative conception of the man. Neither in the end let the reader draw his own moral from the life. Both, in this nineteenth-century sense, "composed" their works.

Both biographers' approaches were closely connected with the biographical and critical doctrines and dogmas of their times, and yet each made his peace with them, and transmuted restrictions into literary power. Southey aimed for example but, by setting his subject's ideal outside the realm of worldly virtues, captured the character and personality together in a brief compass. Lockhart aligned himself with the doctrine of dignity but in doing so was less devoted to the rules of contemporaneous dignity for the sake of distance than he was to the subject's own dignity—a dignity which in Lockhart's hands comes close to tragedy.

Both Southey and Lockhart suppressed: Southey in a single but vitally significant lie, Lockhart in a series of petty misrepresentations, the full significance of which has yet to be unraveled.

Both books have been called masterpieces. That they were written at a time in which nonliterary forces seem to have been more potent and more highly regarded than literary skill, that they found their particular biographical approaches and methods within the scope of contemporary biographical convention, fashion, and dogma are but further testimony to their accomplishment. And they have only to be compared to Moore's *Byron* to reveal how readily either Southey or Lockhart—by following the same rules with a different weighting, or in a rearranged hierarchy of values—could have failed.

CHAPTER EIGHT

SOME PRINCIPLES

This project began with a curiosity about what happened to biography between Boswell and Strachey. The initial assumptions were that, as a peculiarly time-bound genre, biography should develop coherently, changed by its great lights and by trends of contemporary literary history. As Cavendish's *Life of Wolsey* took on the contemporary pattern of the wheel of fortune, and Roper's *More* was hagiography humanized by the English Renaissance, so might Lockhart's *Scott* reflect the Romantic cult of the individual, so would Lytton Strachey signal the end of Victorianism. Historical surveys lead to such fond hopes.

The more biographies I examined, the weaker these assumptions became. The best biographies drew farther and farther away from contemporary lives on the dead-level of biographical practice. They all bore the hallmarks of contemporary mode and dogma, but they seemed to have taken their shape from individual characteristics of biographer or subject, and from individual reactions to contemporary dogma—separate peaces with Mr. Bowdler and Mrs. Grundy. Suppression, produced (it was assumed) by simple prudery, became more understandable, if not more excusable, as a complex combination of Evangelical example-mongering and dignified respect for personal privacy.

Prudery itself did not disappear, but made a more probable case for itself as the nervous anxiety of self-appointed arbiters of morality for the unformed sensibilities of new readers.

Criticism, then, is not simplified by a knowledge of contemporary social history. It is further complicated because no aesthetics has been established for biography. The best biographical criticism has been largely ad hoc: Geoffrey Scott on Boswell and Herbert Grierson on Lockhart designed their principles to explain or to justify their man. Other contributions have been made by intuitive or poetic attempts to define the art: Carlyle's little mirrors for great men and his naphtha lamps of history, Virginia Woolf's granite of truth and rainbow of personality. The ad hoc can suggest useful standards. Geoffrey Scott's principle that the primary truth was the truth of the biographer's mental image, Grierson's suggestion that literal truth is a questionable absolute in biography—both contribute to any critical principles formed after them. The definitions of Carlyle and Mrs. Woolf are perhaps less useful as direct gauges of quality, but they come closer to the heart of an elusive art which must have the poetic quality of suggestion.

I certainly do not wish to attempt a definition of biography here. Biographical criticism already contains entirely too many fallen monuments of abandoned definitions and too few serious explorations of biography's problems. But since this study and its criticism of a few individual lives assume some biographical practices to be good (such as design and economy) and others (suppression and pietistic example) to be bad, some clarification seems necessary to explain the foundations of my critiques.

My first assumption is that biography is an art and not an accident. Macaulay's fallacy—that the subject is the true author of his own biography—seems hardly worth the trouble of refuting: Geoffrey Scott's observations on Boswell have done it in theory, Carlyle's *Sterling* has done it in practice.

Biography's prime value is generally accepted to be a factual narrative which gives a coherent image of one man's life. The second characteristic of all the biographies which have become accepted as landmarks in the art seems to be single authorship.

The work from several hands, although perhaps more efficient as compilation, passes out of the genre. My critiques assume that the proper subject of biography is the single subject, and that the only way to deal with biography as art is to assume that there is an individual acting as the final artistic arbiter of the biographer's flawed freedoms: selection, order, and design.

In exercising his artistic rights, the biographer must keep the man at the center of his book. Any serious departure from this center moves off into informal history; any serious departure from, or changing of, the biographer's donnée of literal truth moves off into fiction.

These artistic freedoms of the biographer are limited by the demands of literal truth. The genre is not primarily of the imagination but primarily of human life—a single human life, lived at one time, and in more or less one place. Resources available to the biographer are all accessible facts, documents, and testimonies concerning his subject's life, and assessments, observations, and narratives of the society and times in which he lived. Selecting from these, and giving them an order, the biographer can employ imagination in arrangement or pattern, suspension, selection, connection, juxtaposition, and balance. Selection is assumed to be necessary. As Carlyle pointed out, exhaustive compilation is good to have, but products of compilation are lives, products of composition, biography.

The coherence and design of a biography depend upon finding a principle or ideal in the man (or in the incidents of his life) which organizes the narrative about it, or a contemporary pattern or design which (although it does not come from within the individual subject) will contain all important characteristics of the subject without omission or distortion. Continually hanging over this organization is the threat of untruth: if the biographer's design is badly chosen, if he neglects important incidents of his subject's history in order to gain greater coherence of design, if he omits facts or categories of factual information, he is subject to the charge of deception. If he omits virtues, he is guilty of vituperation or character assassination; if he leaves out bad qualities, he is a hero worshiper, a sycophant, or a monument builder. The possibilities of failure are really much greater than in a purely imaginative art because of the limitations of factual reality: indeed, if these principles were all applied equally to every case, with no allowance for individual departures for this or that reason, the critic of biography would become like Voltaire's Pococurante, never satisfied, never pleased, never approving. But as the art is flawed, so must the criticism be adaptable. The novelist has available to him all the resources of the imagination and the freedom to invent anything in keeping with his design. To the biographer, only freedom to select, to arrange, and a flawed freedom to depict are available. The biographer's creation must be judged by what he does with available materials.

If we are not to become Pococurantes, we must take what we can get and form our aesthetics upon it. In what direction, then, ought the principles of criticism to be relaxed? Design is necessary. When criticizing Cavendish's *Wolsey*, the critic cannot attack the fallacies of the wheel of fortune, to assert instead that Carlyle's nineteenth-century formulation of the battle of life (man against his society) or twentieth-century psychological assumptions, are fairer, more appropriate, or more realistic. The biographer must be allowed to choose his design, and be granted a certain amount of latitude in its execution. Southey chose to write a brief life, taking his organizing principle from Nelson's writings. Lockhart chose a greater scope, and took a design from contemporary myth. Adapation of plan to subject, of selection to design, of parts to whole, must be the prerogative of the forming hand, if the forming hand is to produce a workable design or, indeed, any design at all.

It is in the hazy regions of truth that relaxation becomes a much more difficult problem. Objectivity in biography is too often oversimplified or dismissed by assertion of one or the other extreme positions on the subject: either the biographer must tell the whole truth, or he must be allowed some of the novelist's freedoms to color or enliven the action. Roy Pascal, in *Design and Truth in Autobiography* (1960), propounded a number of principles formed upon the masterworks of the

golden age of autobiography, the late eighteenth and early nineteenth centuries. Applying these principles to biography produces some useful distinctions between biography and autobiography in the difficult area of the biographer's objectivity,
which is an essential element of the larger question of literal
truth.

Autobiography gives us, Pascal says, the

> inside view, . . . for which the autobiographer is often the
> only authority. But the author himself tends to remain, in
> Henry James' phrase, a "blurred image" in contrast to the
> bright images of the people and things he knows. . . . He
> [the autobiographer] exists for himself as something uncom-
> pleted, something full of potentiality, always overflowing the
> actuality, and it is this indeterminateness and unlimitedness
> that he communicates to us as an essential quality of being.
> The biographer on the other hand works back, inwards,
> from the defined personality, the portrait as it were; realized
> behavior is for him decisive, not the consciousness of poten-
> tiality.[1]

The aim of creation in autobiography, then, is subjective, the
rendering of what it was like to be inside the skin of the author-
subject. The interaction of the autobiographer with his fellow
man must give the determining shape, the "story" of autobiography. Ignoring for the moment Pascal's somewhat limited
assessment of the biographer's method, we may accept that the
biographer aims for the detachment of objectivity; what it was
like to be inside the subject's skin interests him only insofar as
the biographer must use and sometimes explain personal or
autobiographical materials to reach his biographical ends. The
interaction of the subject with his fellow man (strikingly similar
to Carlyle's ne plus ultra for biography) is not the *center* of
biography, but only another measure of courage, integrity, conformity, originality, genius (or the opposites)—in other words,
another measure of character in performance, or perhaps of
personality converted into action. For Boswell, society was the

1. *Design and Truth in Autobiography* (Cambridge, Mass., 1960), p. 18.

setting or, at times, the vehicle for sallies and wit, but the center remained in the whole Johnson, not the social man. For Southey, Nelson's "ungrateful nation" was only one test of the "radiant orb" of honor. For Lockhart, society was Scott's patron and his executioner; in this case, Scott's interaction with his fellows formed a part of the central design, but it was always Scott at the center of that design, not Scott's battle.

Because of the peculiar requirements of autobiography, Pascal sees it as a surpassing art when it achieves its potential.

This is the decisive achievement of the art of autobiography: to give us events that are symbolic of the personality as an entity unfolding not solely according to its own laws, but also in response to the world it lives in. So that these events are symbolic of a whole group of things. Through them both the writers and readers know life. It is not necessarily or primarily an intellectual or scientific knowledge, but a knowing through the imagination, a sudden grasp of reality through reliving it in the imagination, an understanding of the feel of life, the feel of living. . . . The biography, in being more objective, that is, in seeing the person concerned as an object, misses the specific dynamic truth of the autobiography; and we know too how, with the change of time, biographies have to be re-written. There is no tribunal which can deliver a final judgement.[2]

Pascal adds that for autobiography to attain the kind of truth which is its hallmark of greatness, it does not necessarily need to accord itself at every juncture with literal truth.

The distinctions between biography and autobiography here begin to shed some light on the question of literal truth. Truth of the author-subject's emotions is possible and desirable for autobiography; in biography it is not perfectly possible (for the biographer must work with the reflections of the mind, rather than within the mind itself), but a certain consistency of emotional patterns is possible and certainly desirable. They form an important skeletal support to any good biography.

2. Ibid., pp. 185, 195.

Devotion to the literal truth of persons, places, and events is to biography possible (except where limited, in antiquarian lives, by the availability of materials) and necessary; in autobiography, such literal truth is just as possible, but neither necessary nor necessarily desirable. The autobiographer's self-deception concerning those around him may be more informative than his photographic exactitude; the autobiographer emerges through such distortions since they are a part of seeing the world and his friends and enemies through his eyes.

Perfect subjectivity makes selection essential in autobiography: "The numberless impulses and responses of a person have to be reduced to a main strand, and only that which is effective, realised, can be considered worthy of being elaborated."[3] But the pattern derived from reduction to a "main strand" may not, perhaps, represent adequately the views or perspective of a whole life, as it almost certainly takes on the autobiographer's perspective at the time of writing. The pattern is formed by the autobiographer's present; since subjectivity is an aim, this is an asset. For biography, since design may be imposed upon, or derived from, a completed life, or determined anew by the biographer's distanced perspective, and since objectivity is a virtue, dominance of the biographer's estimate of his subject at any one time may be a distracting influence upon his work. The subject's final pose or image of himself, his fame or reputation at death, the impression he made upon the biographer when they first met, when he was younger, or when the biographer was more impressionable—any of these can (and do) take over biographies. To judge the subject by one pose or by one portion of his life is to impose upon the biography the fallacy of the exemplary principle—it is to insist that the man of virtue never slip below the high-water mark of his greatest virtue, that Byron must fail when he is ridiculing his romantic self-concentration. It is to judge the whole by one part, rather than each part by the whole.

3. Ibid., p. 185.

This is not to say that the biographer should remain unmoved by a close association with his subject, for friendship or respect is the most frequent instigator of biography—and friendship or respect frequently is necessarily bound to a particular part of the subject's life: the time of closest association, or the period commanding the greatest respect. Since an essential characteristic of biography is that it be one man's view of another, objectivity will always be somewhat flawed. The biographer chooses his subject because of an attachment. But if this attachment becomes capable of deluding the biographer, if the attachment blinds the biographer to major areas of his subject's character, or if it comes between the biographer's mental image of his subject and the transfer of that image to his book, then the attachment is damaging. To demand total objectivity would be to deny Boswell's attraction to Johnson, Lockhart's to Scott, even Strachey's to Victoria.

The important distinction here between biography and autobiography is that reconstructed objectivity is, on the whole, much more liable to work than reconstructed subjectivity. To reconstruct objectivity, divorced from the dominance of any *now* or *then* view, the biographer has only to work upon his memory and his external emotion; an attempt to reconstruct various moments of subjectivity out of the past would involve more basic evolved principles: intermediate steps of formulation between confusion and a moral, intellectual, religious, or personal solution or compromise. Certainly the autobiography cum journal is a step in the direction of reconstructed subjectivity, but here again as soon as the diary or journal ends, the autobiographer automatically reverts to the *now* subjective. In subjective autobiography, the sympathetic faculty (self-sympathy in this case) could damage the integrity of the *then* emotion. For objective biography, the sympathetic faculty might operate independently—see the *then* emotion as a step to a later result. The autobiographer might not even be aware that a *then* decision was an integral part of an attitude which persisted to death. Thus the autobiographer could habitually assign emotions to the wrong event or person; the biographer would do so only where his information failed him.

This set of distinctions leads to a hierarchy of the kinds of truth in biography. On the lowest level would be literal truth: the facts. This can be compromised, or, to apply a more artistic word (and to put a better color on it), shaped, without essential falsehood, or without destroying or compromising more essential or higher truths. Boswell changes words in Johnson's conversation, Coleridge summarizes his father's table talk, O'Meara remembers as best he can what Napoleon said but has to rush into the next room to dash it off because he doesn't want to write in the presence. These are compromises of the literal truth, but Boswell "Johnsonizes" Johnson, Coleridge's *Table Talk* might well become even duller were it exhaustively complete, and we are grateful to O'Meara for what he offers—none really compromises essential truth, which is truth to the biographer's image, truth to his own objective formulation.

A second level of truth might be established for the faculty of rendering. Using just the literal truth of the facts of a given situation, a writer might put together thousands of situations based upon the same facts, simply by interpreting the surroundings, or the tone of voice, or the expression of a face, or the rendering of physical reality (variant stage productions of any given drama are proof enough of this). Within reasonable limits, this should be a freedom of the biographer, as a function of selectivity. If he does it well, each scene will contribute its part to a whole image of the subject. Boswell strips the setting bare, gives us a few props (a hat, a punch bowl, a cup, a teapot) and renders the scene in accord with his dramatic treatment of all the conversations. Only the essentials are shown on the stage: many of the details are left to Crokers to fill in. Lockhart gives a certain mood to Scott on the battlements of his tower, derived from, and part of, his conception of the whole biography as novel. The setting is important, so we get a sunset, and we get the silences interpreted for us. Betrayal of literal truth is not involved here: these are matters of design and plan. A biography (to paraphrase Nick Carraway) is best looked at through one window after all. It may take in outside testimonies (as both Boswell and Lockhart do) but the organizing view must be unified. Rendering, then, is an area of relative freedom.

Rearrangement and retiming of events is another matter. Certainly Lockhart goes beyond legitimate bounds when he changes dates on letters or sends Scott riding off at night or moves Constable about like king's rook. But aside from lies, or the alteration of dates, quite a bit of freedom ought to be permitted in the timing of a narrative for dramatic or revelatory effect. Again, facts of chronology always weigh it down from soaring off into fiction, but in selection, in the pursuit of individual threads of interest, in the switching back and forth from locale to locale, some freedom and some artistry are required and expected. Day-to-day unfolding of events can make dull reading, and lives are not life: they are an abstraction, an arrangement, an interpretation of life.

The final and most important truth is, of course, the biographer's own truth to his plan, to his image, to his Johnson or his Scott or his Wolsey or his Sterling. Without this the life can become a chaos, a self-contradictory narrative of maybe-this, maybe-that, as incoherent as life itself. Whatever design is chosen, however it is worked out, this truth must lie behind it. We don't read biographies for gossip, and we don't read them just to find out about Mexico or England, or how it was then or how it's changed now. We read for the man in his times— not a man compounded by committee or a man pasted together from his own utterances, but a man seen by one other man, set down as best he knows how.

The biographer's image is the highest truth. The imposition of a nonliterary pattern (such as that of virtuous example), or even of a literary pattern which attempts to make the subject fit a preconceived human or traditional stereotype (as in Moore's theory of genius), can destroy this image. The highest truth depends upon but can easily be destroyed by the facts of literal truth. Slavish loyalty to chronology, to a bulk of facts, or the inability to exclude facts is perhaps the chief source of compromise of image or unity. Image is not reality, nor is it encyclopedia.

The failure of biographer's image can only be determined by literary criticism. It is not an absolute but a relative study, made more difficult by the complexity of a flawed art. The aptness of parts to whole or of design to subject, the completeness of image, are not to be judged by graphs or tables. As Pascal points out (somewhat prematurely and for the wrong reasons), biographies have to be rewritten. This is not because objectivity is marred by closeness of association or because fashion in design of biography changes so sharply with the change of sensibility. Southey's *Nelson* has been rewritten, and the improvement has been, for the most part, by addition to the original or by the restoration of much that Southey excluded in the selections he made from Clarke and M'Arthur's compilation. We can now see more of the design because most of Southey's raw materials are now published. We certainly would read Oman's or Mahan's lives to check a battle, or to find out facts about Lady Hamilton, but we don't necessarily turn to them for reading, or for our image of Nelson. There is a kind of truth in Southey which cannot be improved upon, even if it is not a compendious truth or a complete literal truth. There is also a kind of artistry: treading a narrow path between representation and imaginative creation, between what the man really was and what his biographer sees, between another sort of granite and another sort of rainbow. Basically, biographies have to be rewritten because they are just one man's image of a fellow man: another writer, or another time, brings another image.

Something of this difference between essential and expendable truth is illuminated in James' *Portrait of a Lady*. Madame Merle draws a distinction between the artistic and the artful: "I don't pretend to know what people are meant for; I only know what I can do with them."[4] The good biographer tries

4. Chapter 22.

to get at what his subject was "meant for," the lesser biographer becomes distracted by what he "can do with" him. This is one reason that the critic of biography must often stoop to the intentional fallacy. If the biographer selects for one reason, he is an artist; if for another, he is a sycophant, a liar, an enemy to his art. Criticism, too, must tread a dangerous line of balance. Although Boswell continues to swell the deposit of biographical commentary by virtue of a few ambiguous alterations to old Mr. Hector's account of Johnson as a schoolfellow, the endproduct of his changes amounts to little more than a matter of rendering; but biographical practices prevalent in the nineteenth century have led us to suspect the worst, and suspect it we do.

If the biographer's image of his subject is not derived from the man himself, is not true to the highest objectivity (which corresponds to the biographer's devotion to his mental image of the subject), if he "uses" his subject in the Jamesian sense, then this is a distortion of the highest truth. Thus Carlyle should not be held culpable for seeing John Sterling as a victim of his times, because he is only interpreting or rationalizing his own image of Sterling's life and exercising his donnée of design. Making his subject an example *because* he represents a problem of the times, however, is completely different from making a subject *into* a didactic example to prove this or that point. Robert Huish is culpable for making George IV the perfect gentleman; Roberts is culpable for making Hannah More the perfect humanitarian (despite her more interesting lesser talents); John Watkins is culpable for making Byron the perfect demon. All are bringing the image to the subject and making it fit. All do more damage than Lockhart, with all his "dramatization" of the midnight ride and the touching deathbed. His scenes, lies in themselves, are a part of the truth of an objective image. The distortions of Huish et al. were of the whole, and invalidate whatever facts they may call upon for support.

What a slippery set of principles biographical criticism rests upon. The act of asserting that biography *can* be criticized is only an assertion that Macaulay was wrong, that the discriminating reader prefers form to flux, design to chronology, and composition to compilation. The normal sequence for criticism is reversed. The biographical critic's position is similar to that of the critic of modern tragedy, who does not find Aristotelian characteristics in drama of the twentieth century but knows that, on occasion, something has happened to him in the theater that he identifies with tragedy. Common characteristics must be extracted from all the plays that have this something.

Similarly, the biographical critic must work with what he can get: the ground that is common to Cavendish, Roper, Boswell, Southey, Lockhart, and Strachey. Flawed criticism or appreciative criticism, perhaps, but unless the critic is to narrow his view to parts of a few books or to no books at all, the only criticism possible this side of Macaulay's fallacy.

BIBLIOGRAPHY

Place of publication is London unless otherwise noted.

Allibone, Samuel A., *A Critical Dictionary of English Literature, and British and American Authors . . .*, 3 vols. Philadelphia, Lippincott, 1859–71.

Annual Review; and History of Literature, ed. Arthur Aiken, vols. 1–7, Longmans, 1803–09.

Bates, E. Stuart, *Inside Out: An Introduction to Autobiography*, Oxford, Blackwell, 1936.

Bernard, John, *Retrospections of the Stage* [ed. William Bayle Bernard], 2 vols. Colburn and Bentley, 1830.

Black, John Bennett, *The Art of History; A Study of Four Great Historians of the Eighteenth Century*, Methuen [1926].

Boswell, James, *The Life of Samuel Johnson, LL.D. . . .*, ed. John Wilson Croker, 5 vols. Murray, 1831.

——, *Life of Johnson . . .*, ed. George Birkbeck Hill; rev. ed. by L. F. Powell, 6 vols. Oxford, Clarendon Press, 1934–50.

Bowerman, George F., *The New Biography*, Washington, District of Columbia Library Commission, 1929.

British Museum General Catalogue of Printed Books, 51 vols. Clowes, 1931–54. See below, *Catalogue*.

Bucke, Charles, *On the Life, Writings, and Genius of Akenside; with Some Account of His Friends . . .*, Cochrane, 1832.

Byron, George Gordon, Lord, *Works, Letters and Journals*, ed. R. E. Prothero, 6 vols. Murray, 1898–1901 and after.

Carlyle, Thomas, *Critical and Miscellaneous Essays*, 4 vols. Boston, Munroe, 1838–39.

Carver, George, *Alms for Oblivion: Books, Men and Biography*, Milwaukee, Bruce [1946].

Catalogue of the Printed Books in the Library of the British Museum . . ., 51 vols. republished by the Association of Research Libraries, Ann Arbor, J. W. Edwards, 1946.

Chambers, Robert, *Lives of Illustrious and Distinguished Scotsmen . . .*, 4 vols. Glasgow, Blackie, 1832.

Coleridge, Samuel Taylor, *The Friend*, Penrith, 1809–10.

——, *Specimens of the Table Talk of the Late Samuel Taylor Coleridge* [ed. H. N. Coleridge], 2 vols. Murray, 1835.

Collingwood, R. G., *The Idea of History*, Oxford, Clarendon Press, 1946.

Cook, Davidson, "Lockhart's Treatment of Scott's Letters," *Nineteenth Century*, *102* (1927), 391–96.

Corson, James Clarkson, *A Bibliography of . . . Scott . . .*, Edinburgh, Oliver and Boyd, 1943.

The Critical Review; or, Annals of Literature, Extended and Improved, series II, vols. 31–39; series III, 1–19; series IV, 1–6; series V, 1–2, 4, for W. Hamilton, 1801–16.

Cunningham, Allan, *Biographical and Critical History of the British Literature of the Last Fifty Years*, Paris, Baudry's Foreign Library, 1834.

Dunn, Waldo H., *English Biography*, Dent, 1916.

Durling, Dwight, and William Watt, *Biography: Varieties and Parallels*, New York, Dryden Press [1941].

The Eclectic Review, vols. 19–20, Hodder and Stoughton, 1814.

Edinburgh Review, or Critical Journal, vols. 1–69, Edinburgh, Constable, 1802–39.

Edwards, Edward, and Charles Hole, *A Handbook to the Literature of General Biography*, Ventnor, 1885.

Elliott-Binns, L. E., *The Early Evangelicals: A Religious and Social Study*, Lutterworth Press [1953].

The English Catalogue of Books (Including the Original 'London' Catalogue) . . . Books Issued in . . . Great Britain and Ireland 1800–36, ed. and compiled by Robert Alexander Peddie and Quintin Waddington for the Publishers' Circular, Ltd., 1914.

Fraser's Magazine, vol. 5, Fraser, 1832.

Garraty, John A., *The Nature of Biography*, New York, Knopf, 1957.

The Gentleman's Magazine . . ., vol. 71, parts 1 and 2, Nichols, 1801.

George the Third, His Court, and Family . . ., 2 vols. Colburn, 1820.

Gilbert, Joseph, *Memoir of the Life and Writings of the Late Reverend Edward Williams . . .*, Westley, 1825.

Grierson, Herbert, *Essays and Addresses*, Chatto and Windus, 1940.

———, *Sir Walter Scott, Bart.: A New Life Supplementary to and Corrective of, Lockhart's Biography . . .*, Constable [1938].

Halkett, Samuel, and John Laing, *Dictionary of Anonymous and Pseudonymous Literature . . .*, enlarged by James Kennedy, W. A. Smith, and A. F. Johnson, 7 vols. Edinburgh, Oliver and Boyd, 1926–34.

Haller, William, *The Early Life of Robert Southey, 1774–1803*, New York, Columbia University Press, 1917.

Hart, Francis R., "Boswell and the Romantics: A Chapter in the History of Biographical Theory," *ELH*, 27 (1960), 44–65.

———, "Proofreading Lockhart's Scott: Dynamics of Biographical Reticence," *Studies in Bibliography, Papers of the Bibliographical Society of the University of Virginia, 14* (1961), 3–22.

Hunter, Dard, *Papermaking: The History and Technique of an Ancient Craft*, 2d ed. New York, Knopf, 1947.

Johnson, Edgar, *One Mighty Torrent*, New York, Stackpole Sons [1937].

Johnston, James C., *Biography: The Literature of Personality . . .*, New York, Century [1927].

Knight, G. Wilson, *Lord Byron's Marriage; The Evidence of Asterisks*, Routledge and Kegan Paul [1957].

Lang, Andrew, *Life and Letters of John Gibson Lockhart*, 2 vols. Nimmo, 1897.

Lochhead, Marion, *John Gibson Lockhart*, Murray [1954].

Lockhart, John Gibson, *Memoirs of the Life of Sir Walter Scott, Bart.*, 7 vols. Murray, 1837–38.

Macaulay, Thomas Babington, *Critical and Historical Essays . . .*, ed. F. C. Montague, 3 vols. Methuen, 1903.

Macbeth, Gilbert, *John Gibson Lockhart; A Critical Study*, Illinois Studies in Language and Literature, XVII, 3–4, Urbana, Ill., 1935.

Mahan, Alfred T., *The Life of Nelson, the Embodiment of the Sea Power of Great Britain*, Boston, Little, Brown, 1897.

Malkin, Benjamin Heath, *A Father's Memoirs of His Child* [Thomas Williams Malkin], Longmans, 1806.

Marchand, Leslie A., *Byron: A Biography*, 3 vols. New York, Knopf, 1957.

Maurois, André, *Aspects of Biography*, trans. Sydney Castle Roberts, New York, Appleton, 1929.

Medwin, Thomas, *Journal of the Conversations of Lord Byron: Noted during a Residence with His Lordship at Pisa, in the Years 1821 and 1822 . . .*, Colburn, 1824.

Monthly Review; or, Literary Journal, series II, vols. 34–69, 79–108; series III, vols. 1–15; vols. for 1831–38 (herein designated series IV, vols. 1–24), Henderson, 1801–12, 1816–38.

Moore, Doris Langley, "The Burning of Byron's Memoirs," in *The Atlantic Monthly, 204* (1959), 27–37.

———, *The Late Lord Byron . . .*, New York, Lippincott, 1961.

Moore, Thomas, *Letters and Journals of Lord Byron, with Notices of His Life*, 2 vols. Murray, 1830–31.

———, *Memoirs, Journal, and Correspondence*, ed. Lord John Russell, 8 vols. Longmans, 1853–56.

Nangle, Benjamin C., *The Monthly Review, Second Series, 1790–1815, Indexes of Contributors and Articles*, Oxford, Clarendon Press, 1955.

Neff, Emery, *The Poetry of History: The Contribution of Literature and Literary Scholarship to the Writing of History since Voltaire*, New York, Columbia University Press, 1947.

Nelson, Horatio, Vct., *Letters of Lord Nelson to Lady Hamilton*, 2 vols. Lovewell, 1814.

Nicolson, Harold, *The Development of English Biography*, New York, Harcourt, Brace [1928].

Oliphant, Mrs. Margaret (Wilson), *Annals of a Publishing House: William Blackwood and His Sons*, 3 vols. New York, Scribner's Sons, 1897–98.

Oman, Carola, *Nelson*, Hodder and Stoughton [1947].

O'Meara, Barry Edward, *Napoleon in Exile, or, A Voice from St. Helena: The Opinions and Reflections of Napoleon on the Most Important Events of His Life and Government, in His Own Words,* 2 vols. Simpkin and Marshall, 1822.

Pascal, Roy, *Design and Truth in Autobiography,* Cambridge, Mass., Harvard University Press, 1960.

Peardon, Thomas Preston, *The Transition in English Historical Writing 1760–1830,* New York, Columbia University Press, 1933.

Pearson, Hesketh, *Ventilations: Being Biographical Asides,* Philadelphia, Lippincott, 1930.

Phillips, Lawrence B., *The Dictionary of Biographical Reference . . .,* Philadelphia, Gebbie, 1889.

Plomer, Henry R., *A Short History of English Printing 1476–1898,* Kegan Paul, 1900.

The Quarterly Review, vols. 1–63, Murray, 1809–38.

Rait, Sir Robert, "Boswell and Lockhart," *Essays by Divers Hands,* new series, 12 (1933), 105–27.

Scott, Sir Walter, *The Journal . . ., 1825–26, the Text Revised from a Photostat in the National Library of Scotland,* ed. J. G. Tait, Edinburgh, Oliver and Boyd, 1939.

———, *The Letters . . .,* Centenary Edition, ed. Herbert Grierson, assisted by Davidson Cook, W. M. Parker, and others, 12 vols. Constable, 1932–37.

Sharp, Thomas, *The Life of John Sharp . . .,* ed. T. Newcome, 2 vols. Rivington, 1825.

Simmons, Jack, *Southey,* New Haven, Yale University Press, 1948.

Smiles, Samuel, *A Publisher and His Friends: Memoirs and Correspondence of the Late John Murray . . .,* 2 vols. Murray, 1891.

Southey, Robert, *The Life and Correspondence . . .,* ed. Charles Cuthbert Southey, 6 vols. Longmans, 1849–50.

———, *The Life of Nelson,* 2 vols. Murray, 1813.

———, *Life of Nelson,* ed. E. R. H. Harvey, Macdonald, 1953.

Stauffer, Donald A., *The Art of Biography in Eighteenth Century England,* 2 vols. Princeton, Princeton University Press, 1941.

———, *English Biography before 1700,* Cambridge, Mass., Harvard University Press, 1930.

Strachey, Lytton, *Eminent Victorians,* Chatto and Windus, 1918.

Thayer, William Roscoe, *The Art of Biography,* New York, Scribner's Sons, 1920.

Thompson, James Westfall, and Bernard J. Holm, *A History of Historical Writing,* 2 vols. New York, Macmillan, 1942.

Watkins, John, *Memoirs of Her Most Excellent Majesty Sophia-Charlotte . . .,* 2 vols. Colburn, 1819.

Westminster Review, vol. 28, Baldwin, Cradock, and Joy, 1837.

Woolf, Virginia, *Granite and Rainbow,* New York, Harcourt, Brace, 1958.

INDEX

Abbotsford, 135–36, 149
Abbotsford MSS, 128–29
Abbotstown, 137
Aboukir, battle of, 90
Accumulation, composition by. *See* Biography, misconceptions of
Adam, William, 134
Addison, Joseph, 40
Agamemnon (H.M.S.), 96
Akenside, Mark, 13, 22
Alexander, Emperor of Russia, 8
Alexander, Alexander, 51 n.
-ana, 4
Anecdotes, 4, 11–14, 17, 22 n., 29, 40; popularity in eighteenth century, 24. *See also* Biographical materials, types of
"Anecdote-salvaging," 10–13
Annual Review, 24, 28–29, 31 n., 44, 47, 51 & n., 85
Antiquarian interest of eighteenth century, 12
Applegarth (improver of printing press), 18 n.
Arnold, Matthew, 45, 68, 102
Art books, popularity of, in relation to biography, 25 n.
Atlantic Monthly, 58 n.
Austen, Jane, 24, 136
Authenticity-inclusiveness. *See* Biography, misconceptions of

Autobiography, 157–62. *See also* Biographical materials

Baillie, Joanna, 133
Ballantyne and company, 145
Ballantyne, James, 130, 145–46
Ballantyne, John, 130, 144–46
Barber, Francis, 44 n.
Beaumont, Francis, 113
Beckford, William, 109
Belisarius, 22
Berkenhout, John, 20 n.
Bernard, John, 13
Bernard, William Bayle, 13
Bingley, William, 22 n.
Biographer
  assumes subject's character, 69
  level of talent of, 24
  official, 64
  ownership of materials by. *See* Biographical materials
  qualities of: hero-worship of subject, 8; intimacy with subject, 7; objectivity, 157–62, 165
  roles of: "guardian of the last word," 107, 133–34, 140; "judge" of subject, 28–29, 37
  suitability of, to subject, 21
  as unconscious artist. *See* Biography, misconceptions of
  vision of. *See* Biography, design of

Biographical criticism: general, viii, 154–66; metaphorical figures for biographical art, 77, 79, 100, 155; nineteenth-century: criteria not aesthetic, 18; failed to acknowledge biographer's art, 4–5, 25–26, 48, 66, 72, 79–80, 85, 87; theory, 66–82, 88–89. *See also* Biography, perfectibility of

Biographical dictionaries, 24. *See also* Biography, collective

Biographical materials

obtaining of, 20–21

ownership of: by biographer, 46, 105–06 & n., 107, 127, 152; by family and friends, 48

types of: anecdotes, 12, 71, 87, 92–93, 103, 108; autobiographical items, 42, 85, 87, 89, 130, 133, 156; chronology, 18, 71, 127, 133, 163; conversations, 7–12, 40, 129–30, 134; journals, 42, 46, 60, 105, 111, 132, 140, 147–49; juvenilia, 44; letters, 4, 42, 46–48, 57–58, 65, 83, 89, 92–93, 103, 111, 131–32, 140, 143–47, 149; meditations and prayers, 40, 42, 48–50; memoranda, 42, 44

See also Biographical methods; Biography, design of, misconceptions of, non-literary forces and

Biographical methods: description, depiction, and rendering, 76–79, 157–62; dramatization, 134–35, 138, 140, 151; selectivity, 25, 37, 39, 48, 105, 112, 143–53, 156–57; timing, 25; transcription, accuracy of, 8–9. *See also* Biography, design of

Biography

collective, 25 n.

contemporaneous publication of, 48

criticism of. *See* Biographical criticism

design of, 18, 25, 40, 73, 77, 81, 87, 88–89, 92–101, 104–05, 111–26, 128–29, 133–66; biographer's vision as, 40–41, 88–89, 92–101,
112, 129, 133, 143, 150–53, 155. *See also* Biographical materials; Biographical methods

development of, 3, 154. *See also* historians of

ease of writing, 19

as educational literature, 16. *See also* non-literary forces and, exemplary principle; utility of

eighteenth-century, 15; "absolute faithfulness in representing life," 81; doctrine of dignity, 40; exemplary quality, 28; failure to treat adequately man in society, 81; interest in individual character and personality, 12, 25; minutiae in, 4, 39; popularity of criminal and theatrical lives, 27; trends in, 11

and fiction, 156–57, 163. *See also* Novels

French, 4

historians of, viii, 28, 154

and history, 15–18, 74, 79, 81, 89, 100, 156; as microcosm of the times, 17, 29; individual character as national characteristic, 16; "useful" accessory, 18; relates man to society, 72, 73 & n., 74–75, 81–82, 89, 94, 97–98, 114, 117, 157–58, 165

as "an improving study," 16, 27, 28–37, 49, 62–63, 86. *See also* as educational literature; non-literary forces and

innovation in, vii. *See also* development of

letters considered to be, viii n. *See also* Biographical materials, types of, Letters

mass appeal of, 25–28, 36, 63. *See also* non-literary forces and; Publishing

as "memorial of the dead," 29–30, 31 n., 33–34, 41, 127, 157

misconceptions of: authenticity-inclusiveness, 9–10, 24–25, 32 n., 40, 80, 84, 106–07; biographer as unconscious artist, 6, 37,

66 n., 67, 72, 77–80, 92, 155; biographer's "labors" as compiler, 5, 37, 72, 80, 84; composition by accumulation, 2, 13 & n., 14, 19, 25, 37, 80, 84, 89, 104, 106–08, 125, 142, 156, 163, 166; subject as artist, 4, 5, 18, 37, 66 n., 67, 72, 85, 128, 155, 163 nineteenth-century: popularity of, 25 & n.; quality of, 21; sale of, 86. *See also* non-literary forces and; Biographical criticism non-literary forces and (during the nineteenth century): "author's wishes," 42–45; doctrine of dignity, 4–5, 11, 26, 38–65, 89–90, 102, 107, 129–33, 152; exemplary principle, 26–37, 39, 42, 49, 53, 55–57, 62–63, 68, 87–89, 102, 106, 108, 126–28, 133, 152, 154–57; preservation of "fame and reputation" of the dead, 50, 52, 54, 56, 58–62, 64, 105, 108–11, 129, 160 (see also *De mortuis nil nisi bonum*); family concern, 20, 31, 45, 48, 50–53, 58–65, 100, 102, 105–06, 108, 127, 152; "low curiosity," 16, 33, 41, 47–48, 50 n., 51, 53, 58, 63; new readers, 19, 26–27, 29, 32, 36, 62–65, 155; avoidance of "pain to the living," 47–48, 50, 52, 55, 59–62, 91–93, 100, 106, 108–11, 129–30, 132–33; profit motive—biographies undertaken "to turn a penny," 19, 54–58, 84, 107–08; "public propriety," 4, 62–63, 103, 109–11, 154–55
perfectibility of, 68, 76
as phenomenon of its times, viii, 15, 102, 115, 154
piety, manifestations of, in nineteenth-century, 34. *See also* Biography, non-literary forces and, exemplary principle
popularity of, 25 & n. *See also* mass appeal of; nineteenth-century
prefatory formula for, 31

pre-publication advertisement of, 19
previous falsehood, role of biography in disproving, 45, 103–04, 107–08
privacy, personal, a hindrance to, 38–65. *See also* Biography, non-literary forces, doctrine of dignity
property, literary, in. *See* Biographical materials, ownership of
quantity production of, viii
"Romantic," 28, 154
as "scientific art," 68, 70–71, 81, 159
sub-genres of: criminal lives, 20, 27, 33; deathbed accounts, 8, 20, 35; hagiography, 32, 50, 99–100, 154; scandal, 27, 33; theatrical lives, 27, 32. *See also* Biographical materials
subject of. *See* Biographer
subject matter of: animals, 22 & n.; antiquarian, 22, 24; artists, 36; children, 24, 87; common men, 23, 31; heroes, 21; men of letters, 36
suppression in, 38–65, 91, 108–09, 127, 132–33, 143–56; censorship, 38, 108–09; misrepresentation of facts, 38, 83–84, 90–92, 148–50, 163
as "trash," 44
unity of, 4. *See also* design of; Biographical methods
"utility" of, 16, 44, 49, 62
See also Biographer; Biographical materials; Biographical methods
Black, J. B., 14, 39
Blackwood, Mr., 98
Blackwood, William, 145
Blake, William, 24
Blaquière, Edward, 102
Blessington, Marguerite Gardiner, Ctss. of, 102
Boardman, George Dana, 34
Bolingbroke, Henry St. John, Vct., 16 n.

Bossuet, Jacques Bénigne, 15

Boswell, Sir Alexander (the biographer's son), 131 n.

Boswell, James, ix, 24, 40, 42, 68 & n., 112, 149, 154–55, 158–59, 161–63, 165–66; faith of, in his vision of Johnson, 7; as an "unconscious artist," 6
  works: journals, 134
  Life of Johnson: biographical method of, similarity of Lockhart's to, 133–35, 138, 140, 143, 150
    criticism of, 27; by Carlyle, 71–72, 76–79; in Croker's edition, 3–6; failure to understand, 41; for lack of prudence, 4; by Lockhart, 130–31; by Macaulay, 66–67; nineteenth-century, 46; twentieth-century, 46 n.; by Wordsworth, 47
    imitation of, 7–12; always of parts, not whole, 11
    and nineteenth-century biography, 3, 4 n.
    qualities of: "blanks" in, 6; "breaks through pre-existing delicacies," 47; lack of moral conclusions, 27; minor characters in conversational scenes, 7; "progress toward obscurity," 6
    as a "source of amusement," 4
  See also "Boswell formula"; Boswell Papers
"Boswell formula," 3, 5–7. *See also* Biographical materials, types of, conversations; Biographical methods, dramatization

Boswell Papers, ix, 151

Bowdler, Thomas, 62, 154

Bowhill, 137

Boyer, Abel, 40

Bradford, Grosvenor, 86

British Museum, 67 n.

British Museum Catalogue, 83 n.

Brown, Capt. Thomas, 22 n.

Bruce, John ("John of Skye"), 137–39

Buccleuch, Charles Scott, 4th D. of, 137

Bucke, Charles, 13

Burke, Edmund, 22, 49

Burns, Robert, 41–42, 47, 73, 75

Byron, Annabella Milbanke, Lady, 59–61, 119, 123

Byron, George Gordon, Bn., 10, 24, 38–39, 102–26, 133, 160, 165
  number of biographies of, 22
  works: *Childe Harold*, 103–04; *The Corsair*, 103; *Don Juan*, 103, 121–22, 126; *English Bards and Scots Reviewers*, 121; letters, 103; memoirs, 53, 58–65, 103–04, 107, 125; *Poems . . . on his domestic circumstances*, 120; *Random Thoughts*, 103; *Thyrza*, 116
  See also *Life, Writings, Opinions and Times of . . . Lord Byron*

Cadell Correspondence, ix, 20

Cadell, Thomas, 20–21, 127, 132

Callender, Geoffrey, 83 n.

Campbell, Sir James, 13 n.

Campbell, John, 20 n.

Campbell, Thomas, 21, 48

Caraccioli, Francesco, 95

Carew, Sir Benjamin Hallowell. See Hallowell, Capt. Benjamin

Carlo, the famous dog of Drury Lane, 22 n.

Carlyle, Thomas, vii, 3, 24, 114, 142–43, 155, 157–58
  as biographer, 15, 72 n.
  as critic, 66, 68, 71–82, 156
  criticism, 156
  works: "Biography," 74, 76–78; "Characteristics," 73 n.; "Jean Paul Friedrich Richter Again," 80; "On Boswell's Johnson," 77–79; review of Doering's life of Richter, 2; review of Lockhart's *Burns*, 72 n., 73; review of Lockhart's *Scott*, 80; *Life of John Sterling*, 155, 163

Carter, Mrs. Elizabeth, 44

Cavendish, George, 24, 30, 99, 154, 157, 163, 166

Caxton, William, 18
Charlemagne, 22
Charnock, John, 84
Chatham, William Pitt, E. of, 22
Chatterton, Thomas, 12
Chaucer, Geoffrey, 24, 85
Chaworth, Mary, 117
Chesterfield, Philip Dormer Stanhope, E. of, 16 n.
Chidester, Harriet, ix
Chisman, Sarah, 35 n.
Christ, 22 n.
Christian's Family Library, 25 n.
Chronology. *See* Biographical materials
Churchill, T. O., 84
Churchill, Sir Winston, 65
Clairmont, Claire, 109
Clarke, James Stanier, 53, 84, 88, 164
Clemens, Samuel L., 35
Clifford, James L., ix
Clissold, Henry, 35 n.
Cobbin, Ingram, 35 n.
Cogni, Margarita, 109
Colby, Mrs. David B., ix
Coleridge, Henry Nelson, 10–11, 41, 162
Coleridge, Samuel Taylor, 10, 21, 41, 108–09, 162
Colie, Rosalie, ix
Constable, Archibald, 135, 145, 147–49, 163
Constable's Miscellany, 25 n., 135
Conversation. *See* Biographical materials, types of
Cook, Davidson, 143, 149
Copenhagen, battle of, 93
Corson, J. C., 129 n.
Cowie, Alexander, ix
Cowper, E. (improver of printing press), 18 n.
Cowper, William, 22, 51, 85
Creeger, George R., ix
Critical Review, 65
Croker, John Wilson, 3–6, 24, 42–43, 49–50, 63, 64, 66 n., 71, 131, 162
Cromwell, Oliver, 22
Cunningham, Allan, 27
Currie, James, 52, 75

Dallas, Robert Charles, 126
Dante Alighieri, 112
Davison, Alexander, 94
De mortuis nil nisi bonum, 50–51. *See also* Biography, non-literary forces and, doctrine of dignity
Derncleuch, Kaim of, 137
Description, depiction, and rendering. *See* Biographical methods
Diatesserons. *See* Harmonies of the Gospels
Dickens, Charles, 24, 67 n.
Dickinson, John, 19 n.
Dictionaries, biographical, 24. *See also* Biography, collective
Dictionary of National Biography, 67
Dignity, biographical. *See* Biography, non-literary forces, doctrine of dignity
Dignity of history, 17, 39, 68
Dionysius of Halicarnassus, 16 n.
Documents. *See* Biographical materials
Doering, Heinrich, 2
Don, Sir Alexander, 136
Donaldson, E. Talbot, ix
Douglas, Norman, 65
Dramatization. *See* Biographical methods
Dunn, Waldo H., viii n., 3
Durling, Dwight, viii, n.

ELH, 4 n., 133
East India Company, 136
Edinburgh Cabinet Library, 25 n.
Edinburgh Review, 4, 5, 36, 53, 55–58, 66 n., 72–73, 75, 80, 88
Edleston, John, 115
Egyptians, 30
Eildons, the, 139
Elliott, Mary Belson, 22 n.
Elliott-Binns, L. E., 19 n., 28, 46 n.
English Catalogue, 25 n.
Erasmus, Desiderius, 22
Eulenstein, Charles, 23
Evangelical Movement, 28–37, 46 n., 49, 126, 154

Fair, Mr., 145

Family Library, 25 n., 86 n.
Feidelson, Charles, ix
Ferguson, Sir Adam, 130 n., 136, 138–39
Ferguson, Capt. John, 136
Fiction. *See* Biography, and fiction; Novels
Fitzgerald, F. Scott, 163
Fletcher, John, 113
Florence, Monsieur, 137
Foreign Review, 80
Fornarina, the. *See* Cogni, Margarita
Fox, Charles James, 21
Frederick II (the Great), 22
French Revolution, 15, 115

Gale (publisher), 145
Gale, Curtis, and Fenner (publishers), 67 n.
Gallup, Donald A., viii
Gamba, Count Peter, 102
Garraty, John A., viii n., 28
Garrick, David, 22, 25
Genius, 19th century theory of, 29, 112–26
George III, 13 n., 21, 97
George the Third, His Court and Family (1820), 13, 17
George IV, 21, 55, 133, 165
German, Mrs. Elizabeth, ix
Gifford, John, 20
Gifford, William, 59
Gilbert, Joseph, 31
Glen, James, 130 n.
Godwin, William, 24, 85
Goethe, Johann Wolfgang von, 123; *Werther,* 7
Goldsmith, Oliver, 22, 151
Gospels, as antecedents of biography, 32
Grangerford, Emmeline, 35
Gray, James, 41
Gray, May, 117
Greene, Richard L., ix
Grierson, Herbert, 127, 130 n., 132, 135, 144, 148–49, 155
Griffiths, George Edward, 17 n.
Grundy, Mrs., 154
Guiccioli, Countess Teresa, 109–11

Hagiography. *See* Biography, subgenres
Haller, William, 83 n.
Hallowell, Capt. Benjamin (later Sir Benjamin Hallowell Carew), 95–96
Hamilton, Lady, 53–58, 88, 90–92, 94–95, 98, 164
Hamilton, Sir William, 55, 90
Harmonies of the Gospels, biographical titles of, 22 n.
Harrison, James, 53–54, 84
Hart, Francis R., 4 n., 68 n., 128, 133, 135 n., 144, 146
Hartley, David, 70 n.
Harvey, E. R. H., 83 n.
Haydon, Benjamin Robert, 128
Hayley, William, 51, 85
Hays, Mary, 16 n., 29
Hazlitt, William, 24
Heber, Reginald, 22
Hector, Edmund, 151, 165
Henry V, 22
Henry VIII, 99
Heroes, biographical overtreatment of, 83
Hill, George Birkbeck, 40, 151
Hill, Robert, 92
Hilles, Frederick W., viii, 146 n.
Historiography: personality as shaper of history, 14–18; changes in, 11–18
History
  popularity of, in relation to biography, 25 n. *See also* Biography, history and
Hobhouse, John Cam, 59–61, 106
Hodgson, Francis, 109
Holmes, Mr., of Lyons Inn, 8
Homer, 68, 113
Hope, Thomas, 73 n.
Horton, Wilmot, 60, 61 n.
Howell, John, 51 n.
Huckleberry Finn. See Clemens, Samuel L.
Huish, Robert, 165
Hume, David, 22, 39
Hunter, Dard, 19
Huntly Burn, 136

Hurst and Robinson (publishers), 147
Huston, Benjamin F., ix

Innes, Mr., 144
Ireland, William Henry, 12

James, Henry, 158, 164–65
Johnson, Edgar, viii n.
Johnson, Samuel, 5, 7, 10, 23–24, 31, 44 n., 49, 71, 79, 131 n., 134, 140, 150–51, 165; on biography, 40; Boswell does not imitate style of, 4; *Lives of the Poets*, criticism of, 27. *See also* Boswell, *Life of Johnson*
Johnston, James C., viii n.
Journals. *See* Biographical materials, types of
Juvenilia. *See* Biographical materials, types of

Kean, Edmund, 22
Keats, John, 21, 24
Kemble, John Philip, 22
Kennedy, James, 102
Kernan, Alvin B., ix
King, Alonzo, 34
Knight, G. Wilson, 58 n., 60 n., 62, 108
Koenig steam press, 18

Laidlaw, Will, 128
Lamb, Lady Caroline, 103, 108
Lang, Andrew, 129, 135, 148–49
Lardner's Cabinet Cyclopaedia, 25 n.
Lardner's Cabinet Library, 25 n.
Laura (Petrarch's), 118
Lawrence, Sir Thomas, 21, 48
Leigh, Mrs. Augusta, 60–61, 116–17
Leo X, Pope, 24
Letters, considered to be biography, viii n.; popularity of, in relation to biography, 25 n. *See also* Biographical materials, letters
Lewis, Mrs. Louisa, 134
Library of Congress, 67 n.
Life, Writings, Opinions and Times, of . . . Lord Byron (1825), 102

Literary historians, German, 12
Lochhead, Marion, 3 n., 128–29
Locke, John, 22
Lockhart, John Gibson: criticism, 3, 6; *Life of Burns,* 73, 75; *Life of Scott,* vii, viii, 3, 26, 64, 71, 80, 82, 127–55, 157, 159, 161–63, 165–66
Lockhart, Mrs. Sophia Scott, 135
London and Westminster Review, 80
Long, Edward Noel, 115
Longmans, Rees and company (publishers), 105, 106 n., 145–46
L'Orient (ship), 95
Lovelace Papers, 61
Lovewell, Thomas, 54
Lowe, Sir Hudson, 8
Lowe, Joseph, 17 n.

Macaulay, Thomas Babington, 5, 10, 21, 24, 66–67, 71, 112, 155, 165–66
McCrone, Mr., 129
Macdiarmid, John, 17 n.
MacDougal of Mackerstone, Sir Henry Hay, 136–37
Machine press, advent of, vii
Mackintosh, James, 43
Macpherson, James, 12
Mahan, A. T., 83 n., 164
Malkin, Benjamin Heath, 24
Malkin, Thomas Williams, 24
Man--g, 16 n.
Marchand, Leslie A., 58 n., 59–61, 109 n.
M'Arthur, John, 53, 84, 88, 164
Mathews, Charles, 139
Maty, Matthew, 15
May, John, 86 n.
Meditations. *See* Biographical materials, types of
Medwin, Thomas, 10, 102
Melrose, 139
Melville, Robert Dundas, Vct., 138
Memoranda. *See* Biographical materials, types of
Merle, Madame, 164
Merton, 98–99
Milton, John, 44
Missolonghi, 112

Monthly Review, 5–6, 13 n., 16 n., 17 n., 34, 35 n., 48, 61, 108
Moore, Doris Langley, 58 n., 59, 61–62
Moore, Mary Ann, 23
Moore, Thomas, 38–39, 59–60 & n., 61, 133; *Byron*, vii, viii, 26, 38–39, 58–65, 102–26, 153, 160, 163; *Life of Sheridan*, 105
More, Hannah, 22, 25, 165
More, Sir Thomas, 99, 154
Moses, 22
Murphy, Arthur, 25
Murray, John, 10, 21, 38, 59, 61–62, 86, 105, 106 n.
Murray's Home and Colonial Library, 25 n.

Nangle, Benjamin C., ix, 16 n., 17 n.
Naples, court of, 97
Napoleon Bonaparte, 7–10, 15, 21, 115, 162
National Library of Scotland, 128–29
Nelson, Frances Herbert Nisbet, Ctss., 56, 58, 90–91
Nelson, Horatia, 89 n., 91–92
Nelson, Horatio, Vct., 15, 21, 53–58, 65, 82–101, 104, 114, 136. *See also* Southey, Robert, *Life of Nelson*
Newton, Sir Isaac, 44
Nicolson, Harold, viii n., 28
Nile, battle of the, 97–98
Nineteenth Century, 143
Northcote, James, 36
Novels, popularity of, in relation to biography, 25 n., 32, 36. *See also* Biography and fiction

Ogle, Nathaniel, 22 n.
Ohmann, Richard M., ix
Olin Memorial Library, Wesleyan University, ix
Oman, Carola, 53, 58 n., 83 n., 164
O'Meara, Barry Edward, 7–10, 162

Paley, William, 22
Paper, machine-made, 18
Parry, William, 102
Pascal, Roy, 157–62, 164

Paul, Emperor of Russia, 97
Paul, St., 22
Pennington, Montagu, 44
Petrarch, 118
Pettigrew, Thomas, 58
Pilkington, Mary, 22 n.
Pinto, F. Mendez, 102
Pitt, William, the Elder. *See* Chatham
Pitt, William, the Younger, 20–21, 97–98
Plomer, Henry R., 18 n.
Plutarch, 30
Polton, 135, 149
Pope, Alexander, 112
Pottle, Frederick A., ix
Powell, L. F., 40, 151
Pretyman, George. *See* Tomline, George
Printing, revolution in, 18. *See also* Publishing
Prothero, R. E., 61
Psychology, 46 n., 65, 81, 157
Publication an acknowledgment of truth, 58
Publishers, 19. *See also* Ballantyne and company; Blackwood, William; Cadell, Thomas; Constable, Archibald; Gale; Gale, Curtis, and Fenner; Hurst and Robinson; Longmans, Rees, and company; Murray, John; Rivington and company
Publishing: expansion of, 18–19; payment for biographies, 20–21, 80, 86 & n.; pre-publication advertisement, 48; stock-jobbing of biographies, 20, 37; subscription libraries, 25 n. *See also* Art books; Letters; Novels; Science books; Travel books

Quarterly Review, 3–5, 32 n., 42–43, 49–50, 55, 57–58, 63, 65, 84, 86, 131, 144

Rachel, 22
Rait, Robert, 149
Rattenbury, John, 23

Ravenna, 111
Rees, Owen, 105, 145. *See also* Longmans, Rees and company
Renaissance, English, 154
Reynolds, Sir Joshua, 36
Richardson, Samuel, 95
Richter, Johann Paul Friedrich, 2, 80
Rivington and company, 32
Robert, Nicolas-Louis, 19 n.
Roberts, William, 25, 165
Robertson, William, 39
Robespierre, Maximilien Marie Isadore de, 63–64
Roper, William, 99, 154, 166
Roscoe, William, 24
Rose, Mr., 20
Rousseau, Jean Jacques, 121
Russell, Jane, 147
Russell, Lord John, 60, 105 n., 106

Sacred Classics, 25 n.
San Bartolomeo, 94
San Juan, 94
Sardinia, King of. *See* Victor Emmanuel I
Saturday Review, 65
Schiller, Johann Christoph Friedrich von, 72
Schlegel, Karl Wilhelm Friedrich von, 73
Science books, popularity of, in relation to biography, 25 n.
Scott, Lady, 133
Scott of Darnlee, Dr., 136
Scott of Gala, John, 136
Scott, Geoffrey, 18, 155
Scott, Sir Walter, Bart., 3, 24, 80, 82, 92, 102, 127–53. *See also* Lockhart, John Gibson: *Life of Scott*
Select Christian Authors, 25 n.
Selwyn, George, 12
Shakespeare, William, 22
Sharp, John, 30–32, 45–46, 50
Sharp, Thomas, 30–32, 45–46, 50
Shelley, Mary Wollstonecraft, 109
Shelley, Percy Bysshe, 21, 109
Siddons, Sarah, 22
Sidney, Sir Philip, 102

Simmons, Jack, 83 n., 85
Skene, James, 147
Smith, Nowell C., 42
Smith, Robert A., ix
Smith, Warren H., ix
Smith's Souvenir Classics, 25 n.
Sophia Charlotte, consort of George III, 31, 33
Southcott, Joanna, 23
Southey, Charles Cuthbert, 86 n., 92
Southey, Robert, 24, 103–04; criticism, 29, 51, 84–89, 108; *Life of Nelson*, vii, viii, 26, 64, 71, 82–101, 104, 114, 152–53, 157, 159, 161, 164, 166
Spectator, 65
Stanfield, Clarkson, 67
Stanfield, James Field, vii, 66–71, 73, 75, 77, 80–82, 99, 142
Stanhope press, 18
Stauffer, Donald A., vii, viii, 12, 15, 16 n., 25, 28 n., 31 n., 40, 75 n., 81
Sterling, John. *See* Carlyle, Thomas, works, *Sterling*
Stevenson, Robert Louis, 65
Strachey, Lytton, 14, 154, 161, 166
Studies in Bibliography, 128, 135 n.
Subscription libraries. *See* Publishing
Sunday School movement, 19
Syracuse, 90

Tait, J. G., 147
Tattersall, John Cecil, 115
Temple, Sir William, 40
Teneriffe, 96
Thayer, William R., viii n.
Theological Library, 25 n.
Thwaites, J., M.D., 35 n.
Tomline, George (afterwards Pretyman), 20–21
Trafalgar, battle of, 53, 89 n.
Transcription, accuracy of. *See* Biographical methods
Travel books, popularity of, in relation to biography, 25 n., 32 n.

Vanguard (*H.M.S.*), 90
Venice, 111, 121

Victor Emmanuel I, King of Sardinia, 97
Victoria, Queen, viii, 28, 161
Vindex, *pseud.*, 10
Voltaire, François Marie Arouet de, 14, 22, 39, 121, 157

Walker, Josiah, 75
Walpole, Major General George, 97–98
Walpole, Horace, 12
Walton, Izaak, 24, 30
Warton, John, *pseud.* See Wood, William
Warton, Joseph, 44
Watkins, John, 33, 126, 165
Watt, William, viii n.
Watts, Isaac, 22
Waverley novels, 102
Wellington, Arthur Wellesley, D. of, 15
Werther. See Goethe
Wesley, John, 22
Wesleyan University, ix
Westminster Abbey, 95
Westminster Review. See *London and Westminster Review*

Whittaker's Popular Library, 25 n.
Whitty, Mrs. E., 35 n.
Wilberforce, Robert Isaac, 42–43, 46 n., 49–50
Wilberforce, Samuel, 42–43, 46 n., 49–50
Wilberforce, William, 35 n., 42–43, 46 n., 49–50
Williams, D. E., 48
Williams, Edward, 31
Wilson, James, 23
Wingfield, John, 115
Wolsey, Thomas Cardinal, 24, 99, 154, 157
Wood, William (John Warton, *pseud.*), 35 n.
Woolf, Virginia, 100, 155, 164
Wooll, J., 44
Wordsworth, William, 24, 41–42, 46–47, 50–52, 70, 103, 115, 129–31, 142

Yale Edition of the Private Papers of James Boswell. *See* Boswell Papers
Yale University Library, viii–ix, 20 n., 151
Yorke, Henry Redhead, 20

DATE DUE

APR 1 1 '67			
OCT 3 0 '68			